AMERICA'S SACRED SITES

50 FAITHFUL REFLECTIONS ON OUR NATIONAL MONUMENTS AND HISTORIC LANDMARKS

BRAD LYONS & BRUCE BARKHAUER

chalice press

Saint Louis, Missouri

An imprint of Christian Board of Publication

Interior photo credits begin on page 221.

Front cover photos: New Orleans Jazz National Historical Park photo by Joe Stolarick, USS *Arizona* anchor at Pearl Harbor National Memorial, Statue of Liberty National Monument, and Mount Rushmore National Memorial, all from the National Park Service.

Back cover photos: Golden Gate National Recreation Area photo by Chee Tung, cavate at Bandelier National Monument, and photo by Scott Teodorski of trees in Cumberland Gap National Historical Park, all courtesy of the National Park Service.

Cover design: Brad Lyons, Ponderosa Pine Design. Interior design: Ponderosa Pine Design and Connie Wang. Copyright ©2020. All rights reserved.

ChalicePress.com

Print: 9780827200869

EPUB: 9780827200876

EPDF: 9780827200883

Printed in the United States of America

Dedicated to the American People: You have been given a great legacy, protect it so that your children's children can enjoy it. You have an amazing history. Learn it so that you neither repeat the mistakes of the past nor ignore what gives your country amazing potential. Celebrate the successes, marvel at the beauty, and mourn the failings represented at the sites described on these pages and vow to leave the world better than you found it.

—Bruce

Dedicated to the visionaries, the historians, the artists, the scientists, the teachers, the learners, the preservationists, the activists, the peace-makers, the peacekeepers, the interpreters — to all who teach us the ways of our world and how each of us can make it better.

—Brad

Sunlight at Muir Woods, Golden Gate National Recreation Area

Mission San José, San Antonio
Missions National Historic Park

CONTENTS

Kakaying beneath a rock wall, Pictured Rocks National Lakeshore

Devil's Orchard, Craters of the Moon National Monument and Preserve

ACKNOWLEDGMENTS

Thank you to the families, friends, and mentors who raised us to love nature and history and science and social justice—everything that has aligned to make this book possible.

Thank you to the government photographers for the National Park Service, the National Aeronautics and Space Administration, the White House, and the various researchers for taking and sharing such spectacular images, and to the lawmakers who declared them public domain. Thank you to the webmasters who have built websites with millions and millions of images that take us to all these different places from the comforts of our laptop or smartphone.

Thank you to the volunteers who share their photos through Wikipedia and photo-sharing sites. Unlike *America's Holy Ground,* for which most parks had more images than we could ever need, several parks in this book have photos supplemented by other sources. We are grateful for your artistry and generosity.

Thank you to the team at Chalice Press: Connie Wang for designing these pages, Gail Stobaugh for copyediting, Jim Stropnik for overseeing production of the book you hold, Deborah Arca for shepherding this through the marketing process, and Krista Schaeffer for creating some of the social media. Thanks also to Ulrike Guthrie for editing the original manuscript and Judith Pierson for your copyediting skills.

As always, thank you to those who fought tirelessly to create and sustain these sacred spaces in our country.

Finally, thank you, readers, for your insight, your wisdom, your passion, and your curiosity.

INTRODUCTION

We have all encountered a place where history happened—a place where something or someone started, was born, ended, or died. An event occurred here that changed the course of history. Perhaps it was something enormous, or perhaps it was more simply an observation that was exactly what that person needed *right then* to continue working on a challenge or an idea. Even if that event was long ago, if we're lucky, when we visit that place something in us stirs too, and makes us feel different—maybe a nervous excitement, a subdued dread, or a mind-freeing aha!— and we can feel that God is still working in that very place, years later.

In the United States, many of those important places have been set aside, protected by the National Park Service or its state and local counterparts specifically so that we can experience those moments when we let our guard down, have a heightened awareness, and hear God nudging us in a new direction.

Welcome to *America's Sacred Sites*. We invite you to dig into a National Park Service site from each of the fifty states. We hope you'll travel vicariously through this book and then take it along on your next adventure.

This is the second book through which we invite you to consider and reflect upon the connection between NPS sites and our faith. The first book, *America's Holy Ground*, focused on spaces identified as National Parks, often on the natural beauty and wonder of these places that this country has wisely preserved. National Parks are, by their nature, about nature. Only a few have a human-made centerpiece. Along the way, we offered insight into the history and cultures that embodied these remarkable locations, but it was the splendor and majesty of the spaces themselves that captured our imaginations and revealed something of the mystery of our Creator in our chosen themes for each space.

America's Sacred Sites is similar, but different. As we continue exploring the vast and varied array of places related to the National Park Service, our focus shifts to the significance of events at a particular location, rather than simply its God-given beauty. The scale changes from thousands of square miles containing rivers and mountains and bears and birds to places the size of a family home. The importance of the place, however, is not size, but the significance of what happened on or near that space.

The sacred and sometimes the profane are revealed not only in the earth's beauty but also in the events that shape a country and its people. Here, memory plays a role in calling us to recall, with celebration or mourning, the marks we have inscribed upon the time line of our nation's story. The events sometimes define us at our best and at our worst. The locations can inspire our idealism and testify to our grandest aspirations, or remind us who we have struggled to be, to remain, or to become.

To illustrate our intention, consider the stories in the biblical witness where a place is marked as special or sacred. In Genesis 12, when Abram enters Canaan, God having told him in a dream that he and his descendants will one day inhabit this land, Abram sets up a pile of stones—an altar—at the oak of Moreh. The place is to be remembered

Harpers Ferry, West Virginia

because something out of the ordinary happened there. In this case, it was the first concrete step of Abram living into the vision of what would become the biblical nation of Israel. Marking the place allows the history to live on beyond the individual or generation that experienced the event.

North American porcupine, Knife River Indian Villages National Historic Site, 2016. North Dakota

While different cultures might remember an event associated with a place or object, they may not share a common view of what that memory means. Palestinians, for example, view Abraham's first footfall on the land of Canaan very differently than modern-day Israelis. Native Americans view Christopher Columbus and the "discovery" of the New World very differently than do people of white, Anglo-European descent. These two perspectives, vastly different in almost every way, share the same moment in history and a spot on the map.

Mosquito Lagoon at Canaveral National Seashore, Florida

Sometimes the place and the event are so interwoven that they are synonymous. Golgotha seemingly cannot be separated from the crucifixion of Christ, just as the Edmund Pettus

11

Tripod Practice, Mount Rushmore in South Dakota

Bridge in Selma, Alabama, and the galvanization of the civil rights movement in the United States are inseparable.

Many of the places in this book can be interpreted in multiple ways. We are bound to have missed a few.

What piqued our interest was to reflect upon a place, a date, an event, or an object that engages not only our sense of being an American, but also of being a person of faith. How was God, how were God's people perceived as present—or perhaps absent—in what happened in this particular place and moment? Do certain events cause us to reflect more deeply upon our faith and how it calls us to be citizens in two worlds? How does following the God of the Abrahamic traditions invite us to think critically about our own history? How does such a call invite us to discover our better natures and our hope for realizing a fuller expression of our values and ideals—ideals with foundations in justice, equality, and the pursuit of individual happiness in communal relationships?

Not all of the places, events, objects, or dates mentioned in *America's Sacred Sites* demand a complex evaluation of our shared history. There are still places of wonder, such as Devils Tower National Monument and Knife River Indian Villages National Historic Site. There are celebrations of achievement remembered in places like the Wright Brothers National Memorial, or Canaveral and its National Seashore. There are symbols that we share, like the Liberty Bell, the Statue of Liberty, and Mount Rushmore.

There are places that inspire us. New England's National Park Service units focus on artists. Nicodemus National Historic Site introduces us to African Americans who went west in hopes of finding a better life after emancipation. And the country's most-visited national park site, Golden Gate National Recreational Area, reminds us that we need to unwind every now and then.

But a faithful and faith-filled look at ourselves also requires that we visit sites that recall our country's hardest times, such as Harpers Ferry, the Selma to Montgomery National Historic Trail, and the Oklahoma City National Memorial. All of these places, symbols, and events, for both the courage and the violence exhibited there, make us who we are as Americans in the early twenty-first century.

What is most remarkable to us is that there is a place in every state of our union that has some significance in shaping us and our history. Consequently, there is a place near you right now where a visit can get you started on discovering more of America's holy ground. We wish you blessings and safe as well as amazing journeys as we remember that our memories of the past, well-tended, not only define who we are now, but can shape us into something even greater in our shared future.

Devils Tower, Wyoming

INVOCATION

"Then [God] said, 'Come no closer! Remove the sandals from your feet,
for the place on which you are standing is holy ground.'"
—Exodus 3:5 (NRSV)

"Here is your country. Do not let anyone take it or its glory away from you.
Do not let selfish men or greedy interests skin your country of its beauty, its riches
or its romance. The World and the Future and your very children shall judge you
according to (the way) you deal with this Sacred Trust."
—President Theodore Roosevelt

"We are not makers of history. We are made by history."
—Martin Luther King Jr., US civil rights movement leader

"History, despite its wrenching pain, cannot be unlived, however,
if faced with courage, need not be lived again."
—Maya Angelou, US author

"Sometimes history takes things into its own hands."
—Thurgood Marshall, US attorney and Supreme Court justice

"As we Americans celebrate our diversity, so we must affirm our unity if we are
to remain the 'one nation' to which we pledge allegiance. Such great national
symbols and meccas as the Liberty Bell, the battlefields on which our independence
was won and our union preserved, the Lincoln Memorial, the Statue of Liberty,
the Grand Canyon, Yellowstone, Yosemite, and numerous other treasures of our
national park system belong to all of us, both legally and spiritually.
These tangible evidences of our cultural and natural heritage
help make us all Americans."
—Edwin C. Bearss, National Park Service Chief Historian,
1981–1994

"History is who we are and why we are the way we are."
—DAVID McCULLOUGH, HISTORIAN AND AUTHOR

"Sacred means different things to different people. And to the American Indians, sacredness means everything was alive. The trees, the rocks, everything inside where we now have national parks had a spirit. And that was the sacredness. They came there to learn, they came there to pray. Now you can go in there and you can walk as our ancestors did. You can go in there and you can see what the Creator has made for us. And things are alive. You can feel it, you can feel the spirits."
—GERALD BAKER, MANDAN-HIDATSA AND NPS SUPERINTENDENT

"More and more as we come closer and closer in touch with nature and its teachings are we able to see the Divine and are therefore filled to interpret collectedly the various languages spoken by all forms of nature about us."
—GEORGE WASHINGTON CARVER

"Nature is ever at work building and pulling down, creating and destroying, everything whirling and flowing, allowing no rest but in rhythmical motion, chasing everything in endless song out of one beautiful form into another."
—JOHN MUIR, US NATURALIST

"Travel is fatal to prejudice, bigotry, and narrow-mindedness."
—MARK TWAIN, US AUTHOR

"Before the mountains were born
or you brought forth the whole world,
from everlasting to everlasting you are God. . . .
A thousand years in your sight
are like a day that has just gone by,
or like a watch in the night."
—PSALM 90:2, 4 (NIV)

Dignitaries cross the Edmund Pettus Bridge during celebrations marking the march's fiftieth anniversary.

SELMA TO MONTGOMERY NATIONAL HISTORIC TRAIL

ALABAMA • 1996 • PROGRESS

Here there is no Gentile or Jew, circumcised or uncircumcised, barbarian,
Scythian, slave or free, but Christ is all, and is in all.

—COLOSSIANS 3:11 (NIV)

Slavery, oppression, poverty, the stripping of basic American rights, being denied the vote—so many indignities were forced on African Americans for centuries. But the civil rights movement of the 1960s focused on the South, where violence made the struggle for equality especially dangerous.

In 1965, the killing of Jimmie Lee Jackson, shot in the stomach while trying to protect his mother from the blows of an Alabama state trooper's night stick, demanded a public response. A march from Selma, Alabama, to the state capitol in Montgomery, fifty-four miles east, would bring international attention to the plight of African Americans in the South, another step in the civil rights movement. A coalition of peaceful civil rights groups, with leadership from Dr. Martin Luther King Jr., organized the march.

Two weeks after Jackson's death, it was a small group that set out for Montgomery the first time on March 7, 1965, but one that had garnered the attention of the national media. After crossing the Edmund Pettus Bridge, the group was met by state police and a deputized mob equally determined that there would be no march. With little warning the mob charged the unarmed group with billy clubs, tear gas, and even pieces of furniture wrapped in barbed wire, and beat the marchers mercilessly, driving them back and pursuing them toward the Brown Chapel AME church where the march had begun.

The events of that day became known as Bloody Sunday. As these

Alabama State Police confront marchers and order them to disperse.

events came into the nation's living rooms on the evening television news, it galvanized the push for civil rights protections across the country. In the initial blockage of the march, the civil rights movement won a substantial victory. "What clashed that day were not competing armies," said President Barack Obama at a ceremony marking the march's fiftieth anniversary, "but competing ideas about the vision and direction of this country." When the march crossed the same bridge ten days later, over twenty-five thousand people shared in making progress toward the highest ideal of our founding documents—that all people are created equal.

Between Selma and Montgomery, US 80 passed impoverished small towns and unforgiving land once farmed by slaves and sharecroppers, reflecting the history of isolated rural black America with lower educational achievement, bypassed economic progress, high unemployment, and limited opportunity for the advancement of its inhabitants or their descendants. Today, though, there are sacred spaces amidst the profane legacy of racism, spaces that testify that this road represents a moment when the embedded systemic mechanics of oppression were not simply a *black* problem, but our *national* problem, worthy of the ultimate sacrifice, if necessary, to right the pervasive oppressions. This road is not simply paved with asphalt but with the blood, pride, and moral fortitude of a country.

Pause along the route to visit the memorial to James Reeb and the gravesite of Viola Liuzzo, who died at the hands of the Ku Klux Klan. Linger where the march stopped to rest and imagine the strange mixture of fear and adrenaline that accompanies acting on your deepest convictions, worth any cost imaginable.

The march hastened the passage of the Voting Rights Act of 1965, and it bore witness that the power of democracy and the great experiment of self-governance that is these United States is founded on the right to vote. It acknowledged that government is merely veiled tyranny without this right for *all*. It validated the power of peaceful nonviolent protest to effect change.

What was won in the Selma-to-Montgomery march was not an eradication of bigotry and injustice. The bill didn't end oppression and racism; it simply denied it the protection of the law. Racism and the fight to end its ugly scourge continue. There are still those who deny equality to some. Progress has been made, but more is needed.

The author of Colossians believed that God makes no distinction regarding race, gender, or social status, and thus this National Historic Trail reminds us of the need to carry the values of our faith into the political arena so that God's will can be done on earth as it is in heaven. Our efforts to live out these values may be one marker of the progress of our faith journey.

What does "created equal" mean to you? When have you advocated for the rights of others? When has someone fought on behalf of your rights?

Martin Luther King Jr. and marchers arrive at the Alabama State Capitol on March 25.

KLONDIKE GOLD RUSH NATIONAL HISTORICAL PARK

ALASKA AND WASHINGTON • 1976 • ADVENTURE

In hard traveling year in and year out, I've had to ford rivers, fend off robbers,
struggle with friends, struggle with foes. I've been at risk in the city,
at risk in the country, endangered by desert sun and sea storm, and betrayed by
those I thought were my brothers. I've known drudgery and hard labor,
many a long and lonely night without sleep, many a missed meal,
blasted by the cold, naked to the weather.

—2 Corinthians 11:23–27 (Message)

Few ideas have been romanticized more in American lore than the idea of setting out on an adventure and striking it rich—striking gold.

California is the prime example of a place that exploded because of a gold rush, in part because the land stormed by the forty-niners held riches beyond their imaginations. That's not true of the Klondike Gold Rush five decades later, which promised riches but proved a colossal bust. In August 1896, three men discovered gold in a tributary to Canada's Klondike River. By the time word of the find got back to civilization, the prime sites had already been snapped up, but that didn't stop tens of thousands of prospectors from catching the first available ship out of Seattle and heading north.

Those ships often docked in Skagway, perched precariously on the edge of the Taiya Inlet, an inhospitable place whose very name refers to rough seas in the local Tlingit language. Skagway was a rough-and-tumble boomtown overwhelmed by the sudden crush of miners heading north.

In light of the extremely hostile land awaiting them, prospectors were required by Canadian authorities to take a year's worth of

Looking toward the 1,500 "Golden Steps" up Chilkoot Pass

Prospectors lugging their packs over the pass

supplies with them— no easy task: food alone weighed half a ton, plus another half-ton of supplies. That would be tough to transport on level land, about thirty-five miles as the crow flies. But all those supplies, every single ounce, had to be transported to the Klondike's headwaters, up and over Chilkoot Pass (3,759 feet) or White Pass (2,864 feet), without the aid of automation. Moving a ton of supplies required many, many trips, averaging three months' work; those who successfully transported all their gear had therefore hiked more than a thousand miles before finally setting out for the gold fields six hundred miles downstream. At least it was all downhill from there.

Photos from the Klondike Gold Rush show ant-like lines of prospectors trudging up the slopes. Many died in the effort, from the work, disease, avalanches, the cold, or for more nefarious reasons. Thousands of pack animals perished too. It was brutal work, yet up to thirty thousand miners made the trek in the rush's first year.

The Klondike Gold Rush was, indeed, a flash in the pan; another gold find further west in Alaska led to the end of gold fever in the Klondike. Very few miners made any kind of fortune. But those who survived had a heckuva story to share!

Nowadays, Skagway is a picturesque tourist town popular with mammoth cruise liners touring the coast of southeast Alaska and British Columbia. More than a million people visit Skagway each year to see dozens of buildings dating back to the rush. Tour buses transport tourists up the winding Klondike Highway, completed in 1978, into the Klondike Country and beyond. Across the valley, the White Pass and Yukon Railroad retraces the railroad, completed just as the gold rush petered out.

If another gold rush were to erupt today, a ton of food and supplies could be piled into a trailer and hauled over White Pass before you finish your morning coffee—though the spectacular views of the Coast Mountains, the glacier-carved lakes, and the stark, surreal landscape around you will probably slow you down as you savor every scenic overlook. When you're done prospecting, your drive back to Seattle would only take two or three days, depending how much you want to drive in a day.

In the humdrummery of our daily lives, it's easy to fall into a routine, to get bored. Try as we might, it happens at work, at home, and in our relationships with family and friends and those we love. Adventure—breaking the routine, doing something that energizes you—adds spice to our lives. Everybody needs a little adventure now and then. Not necessarily a gold rush, of course.

What is the greatest adventure you've had in your life? What adventure is brewing in your own life, in your town, or elsewhere in the world? With whom do you want to share your adventure?

Fuschia fireweed and inuksuk, rock piles that told travelers
they were on a path others had traveled before

TUZIGOOT NATIONAL MONUMENT

Two are better than one, because they have a good return for their labor:
If either of them falls down, one can help the other up.
But pity anyone who falls and has no one to help them up.
Also, if two lie down together, they will keep warm.
But how can one keep warm alone?
Though one may be overpowered, two can defend themselves.
A cord of three strands is not quickly broken.
—ECCLESIASTES 4:9–12 (NIV)

"If you want to go quickly, go alone," says an African proverb. "If you want to go far, go together." Life in the desert is difficult and it is hard to imagine going it alone. This would have been particularly true in the prehistoric southwestern United States. Survival depended on resources like food and water, easier to gather by collaboration than self-reliance. The formation of communities allowed for the development of a social stratification that enhanced each member of the group, designating skilled persons to perform select duties, which divided the labor and allowed for additional and more diversified skill sets to emerge.

At a basic level, having a select group of hunter/gatherers allowed other members of the group to manage higher-level tasks, such as shelter construction, food preparation, or making clothing. Eventually craftsmen and artisans emerged to engage in pottery making, beadwork, and tool manufacturing with the available natural resources that became the economic instruments for bartering and trade.

High on a hill outside of what is modern-day Clarksdale, Arizona, stands the Tuzigoot Pueblo, evidence of a community of Sinagua people who inhabited the space between 1000 and 1400. The Sinagua

A look at the communal nature of Tuzigoot's construction

Reconstructed pottery from the Tuzigoot community

(meaning "without water") were a pre-Columbian people who occupied the central Arizona region around what is now Flagstaff, Sedona, and the Verde Valley.

Excavations tell the story of a people who lived together in a structure similar to an apartment complex, rather than in individual dwellings. Square rooms were created by piled rock held together by clay mortar, dug into the hillside, and sharing a set of common interior walls. At its peak, it is estimated that as many as 250 people lived in the pueblo, which appears to have grown over time.

Despite the name *Sinagua*, the Tuzigoot community had access to water from the Verde River, which flows below the pueblo to the south and at Peck's Lake to the north. This location also provided rich resources of copper ore, salt, and minerals including malachite, azurite, and argillite. But the excavation also shows a vast store of goods: pottery from many different but related cultures spread across the Coconino Plateau and Hopi Mesa; obsidian projectile points from north of the San Francisco peaks; and Scarlet macaws from Mexico. This suggests that Tuzigoot was perhaps the center of a vast trading network between desert communities.

Tuzigoot is identified in some Hopi histories, suggesting it was not only a community with highly socialized trading skills but also a place where migrating clans coming from the south may have stayed or temporarily settled as they moved through the Verde Valley. The people who lived there apparently valued hospitality, as they welcomed those migrating from other parts of the desert and understood the mutually beneficial value of these relationships.

Building a community benefits its members. Drawing from diverse gifts, the influence of differing ideas, and a competitive nature that strives to be the best can all contribute to forging the common good and the enrichment of the collective whole. Given the character of human beings, maintaining a sense of community is not always easy. The differences that strengthen can also become points of contention. Yet, despite this, the advantages of functioning together outweigh the trouble and effort.

The writer of Ecclesiastes expresses the potency of choosing to live in community over and against remaining alone. For all of our Western civilization's ideas about independence, self-determination, and self-reliance, there is no doubt that without interdependence, communal accountability, and a mutual embrace of "the other" our human achievements would be limited and our individual success stifled. Even when the people of Tuzigoot abandoned the pueblo for reasons that are unclear, it appears that they chose to leave together.

What does *community* mean to you? What are the difficulties you face in choosing to live/work with others? How are you different (or perhaps more complete) by being with others?

The size and scale of the site is best discovered from a distance.

Little Rock Central High School's elegant architecture

LITTLE ROCK CENTRAL HIGH SCHOOL NATIONAL HISTORIC SITE

ARKANSAS • 1998 • COURAGE

Nebuchadnezzar said to them, "Is it true, Shadrach, Meshach and Abednego, that you do not serve my gods or worship the image of gold I have set up? . . . If you do not worship it, you will be thrown immediately into a blazing furnace. Then what god will be able to rescue you from my hand?" Shadrach, Meshach and Abednego replied to him, "King Nebuchadnezzar, we do not need to defend ourselves before you in this matter. If we are thrown into the blazing furnace, the God we serve is able to deliver us from it, and he will deliver us from Your Majesty's hand."

—DANIEL 3:14–17 (NIV)

Imagine: You will go to a place where you are not wanted. Some people will threaten to kill you just for being there. They will say cruel things about you and those you love. You will be the focus of international curiosity and debate. Some will call you a hero, others will call you unspeakable names. You will have protection, but there is no way to know if that protection will be enough. There is no guarantee that any of what you are about to experience will end well.

Also, you're a teenager.

Would you have been up to the challenge?

Little Rock Central High School National Historic Site honors both the nine African American students who had the courage to integrate a white school and those who helped desegregate a school district and the nation, whether by their own choice or by following orders with which they did not necessarily agree.

The most expensive high school in the country when it was finished in 1927, Little Rock Central is today a beautiful, stately structure with broad, inviting steps, a reflecting pool, and elegant architecture evoking classical cathedrals and the contemporary Art Deco of its youth. Over the main entry doors loom four gleaming white statues representing ambition, personality, opportunity, and preparation—all qualities that would be needed by its students in 1957.

In May 1954, the Supreme Court ruled in *Brown v. Board of Education of Topeka,* Kansas, that American public schools must be racially integrated. Reaction to the decision was mixed all over the country, not just in the South. Little Rock conceded to integrate, beginning with its high schools, at the beginning of the 1957 school year. Nine students (six females, three males) were selected to attend Central that fall: Minnijean Brown, Elizabeth Eckford, Ernest Green, Thelma Mothershed, Melba Pattillo, Gloria Ray, Terrence Roberts, Jefferson Thomas, and Carlotta Walls. They became known as the Little Rock Nine.

Soldiers protect the Little Rock Nine on the high school's steps.

Outraged, Arkansas Governor Orval Faubus mobilized the Arkansas National Guard under the pretense of preserving the peace. But the aggressive message of armed soldiers on the school lawn was clear: Faubus planned to keep Little Rock segregated. A litany of court actions gave victories to both integrationists and segregationists, but as the school year approached, the Little Rock Nine were on a collision course with history.

On September 23, 1957, the nine students arrived for classes, mobbed by a thousand furious protestors. The Little Rock Nine didn't complete the school day, removed for their own protection by Little Rock police. Recognizing the volatile situation, President Dwight

Eisenhower took control of the national guard and ordered the army to the scene. Two days later, protected by the 101st Airborne Division, the Little Rock Nine reentered the school and began classes.

Testament: The Little Rock Nine Monument sculpture by John Deering, Kathy Deering, and Steve Scallion at the Arkansas State Capitol

Later that academic year, Green became the school's first African American graduate, but segregationists kept fighting. The following year, 72 percent of Little Rock voters cast ballots to keep schools segregated. Eventually, after years of conflict, integration became the norm, the protests died down, and Little Rock Central began its new life as an integrated school.

The Little Rock Nine went on to their own accomplishments. Most graduated from Central, and all graduated from college; they became teachers, public servants, journalists, social workers, and a scientist, and many continued their work for the greater good. Just as Shadrach, Meshach, and Abednego mustered the courage to confront Nebuchadnezzar, putting their lives on the line, the courageous Little Rock Nine inspired others to take their own stands, changing our country one institution at a time.

What is the most courageous act you have ever undertaken to serve others? What do you wish you had the courage to do today? How do you help others find courage to do the nearly impossible?

The Marin Headlands, Golden Gate Bridge, and San Francisco

GOLDEN GATE
NATIONAL RECREATIONAL AREA

CALIFORNIA • 1972 • FUN

There's a season for everything
and a time for every matter under the heavens . . .
a time for crying and a time for laughing,
a time for mourning and a time for dancing.
—ECCLESIASTES 3:1,4 (CEB)

Where do you go to have fun? For millions of people each year, the answer is a national park site. But it may not be the particular national park that first springs to mind. It's not Great Smoky Mountains, the most visited of the sixty-one national parks, or the monuments in the nation's capital, but Golden Gate National Recreation Area.

More than fifteen million people visit Golden Gate each year. The metropolis around San Francisco Bay is the country's fifth largest metropolitan area with almost ten million residents, and it is a popular tourist city at home and abroad. With locations stretched over nearly sixty miles along the Pacific coast, the park can be a destination after a busy workday or part of an epic road trip.

Looking for a natural getaway from the fast-paced city? Muir Woods is the legendary home of old-growth coast redwoods, towering over trails that wind through a carpet of ferns and other plants that are part of a mammoth natural recycling factory. Reaching over 250 feet high, the redwoods here are around seven hundred years old, still young for a tree known to live more than two millennia. Or head for the beaches and feel the sand around your feet. From the Marin Headlands, take in the world-famous view of the city before you set out for Gerbode Valley's grasslands, wildflowers, and chaparral. If you want to stay in the city, Land's End provides sweeping views of both Golden Gates—the bay's

Beneath the redwoods in Muir Woods

entry and the bridge that spans it.

How about history? Learn about the early Spanish settlers and see how the American military protected this vital port, from early territorial forts to a deactivated Cold War-era Nike anti-bomber missile. Fly a kite or work on your tan at Crissy Airfield, a key training site in the early days of aerial defense. A mile offshore sits one of the park's best-known landmarks—Alcatraz Island, the famous prison that imprisoned the most troublesome inmates in federal custody. A prison tour can be a fun diversion, including its tourist-trap aspects and the inevitable jokes about locking up random tourists, but it's also a lesson in the civil rights movement. Tours recall the nineteen-month-long occupation of Alcatraz by Native American rights activists.

For budding scientists, the Marine Mammal Center and Bay Area Discovery Museum provide a new perspective on our surroundings and are kid friendly. Explore the airfield's successful restoration effort that resulted in many fish and bird species making their homes in the area, along with more than one hundred species of native plants.

And it's impossible to ignore the enormous red bridge at the

Alcatraz Island and the Bay Bridge

center of the park, with its elegant lines and mind-boggling engineering. While it's not part of the park, the Golden Gate Bridge is still a magnificent, majestic masterpiece. It's hard to look away from the landmark, and a trip to San Francisco doesn't feel complete until you've passed under its twin towers.

If any park can boast to have something for everyone, Golden Gate may be it. It claims thirty-seven different sites that sound like a complete vacation package.

However, we don't need to have the country's most popular park in our backyard to break up the routine of everyday life. It doesn't require a trip to San Francisco or a national park or even a local park. Catching a movie or a concert, cooking a favorite recipe or a new one, taking the long way home from work, chatting with a friend, playing with the dog—we have so many ways to take a break, get our minds off our troubles, and catch our breath. We humans are meant to have fun—alone or with others, friends and strangers alike. And we benefit from the new perspective to think about our faith, about the way we interact with each other, about the way we live our lives, and about what we believe.

What habits of yours could you change to have more fun? Who are the people in your life with whom you enjoy spending time, and why? What is on your list of things you still want to try or experience?

Wildflowers at Mori Point

DINOSAUR NATIONAL MONUMENT

"I establish my covenant with you: Never again will all life be destroyed by the waters of a flood; never again will there be a flood to destroy the earth."
And God said, "This is the sign of the covenant I am making between me and you and every living creature with you, a covenant for all generations to come: I have set my rainbow in the clouds, and it will be the sign of the covenant between me and the earth."
—GENESIS 9:11–13 (NIV)

One day long ago, everything changed. The inhabitants of our planet likely were not intelligent enough to recognize that change was happening, nor were they able to do anything about it. That change affected some inhabitants immediately, while it took generations to affect others. What we know for sure is that dinosaurs, once the most sophisticated creatures on our planet, either changed as a creature to become something different, or they perished, never to be seen alive again.

We know this because the earth has a miraculous way of telling its story. Geology preserves history in its layers of rock, capturing pieces of history within rock for a long, long time. We see these layers when we encounter places where water or wind or technology have cut through the rock or where earth itself has broken, exposing its history. We see history in the chemicals trapped in the rock. We detect a different atmosphere in those rocks, reflecting how life was so much different on our planet, how temperatures changed, and what other vapors were common at that time. And in a few rare places, we can see evidence of long-gone life itself entombed in the rock.

Dinosaur National Monument is among the world's best locations to see fossils of the captivating creatures and to learn more about what this

Mitten Park Fault and the Green River

Camarasaurus skull

planet was like long, long ago. Straddling the Colorado-Utah border, the monument embraces the Green and Yampa River valleys. Cutting down through sedimentary rock, the rivers reached 150-million-year-old sandstone and its treasure trove of Jurassic-era dinosaur bones. Native Americans have been in the area for thousands of years, but only in 1909 did paleontologist Earl Douglass begin excavating the find.

The rocks at Dinosaur have preserved many species of dinosaurs, with scientific names that are tough to spell or even pronounce, unless you're that four-year-old dinosaur expert who knows each species by memory. You may recognize the meat-eating, pack-hunting *Allosaurus* from your nightmares, with its three-inch-long serrated teeth and hooked claws. *Stegosaurus* is easy to spot thanks to the vertical plates atop its spine and its spiky tail. *Deinonychus* and its seventy teeth could rapidly devour its prey in a manner very similar to the raptor birds we see today. The plant-eating *Diplodocus* could be ninety feet from head to tail but was light by dinosaur standards, weighing in at around fifteen tons. Its cousins, *Camarasaurus,* have oddly square-shaped skulls and ate rougher foliage. Fossils of these creatures, as well as smaller animals that lived beside them, are entombed in the rock where they fell long ago. Paleontologists still unearth new discoveries; a new species, plant-eating *Abydosaurus*, was unearthed in 2010.

Cliffs towering over the Yampa River

All this is possible because of the geological process that lays down soil over soil, compacting it to rock sturdy enough to protect the fossils but also pliable enough to be eroded. Every step we take is upon the newest layer of soil, which may someday become rock buried hundreds or thousands of feet below where our descendants will walk. What story will they find when they encounter our own fossils? What of our life will be preserved, and what will be recycled in our planet's amazing life cycle?

Dinosaur National Monument itself required preservation in the 1950s. Even though the monument was among the first federally protected sites, the US Bureau of Reclamation proposed a dam that would have flooded the valley. With echoes of the early national park battles that resulted in the damming of Yosemite National Park's Hetch Hetchy Valley but the sparing of Kings Canyon National Park, Dinosaur was saved by a political compromise that allowed other dams but also set a precedent for preservation of protected lands in a battle that continues to this day in other federally protected areas. Dinosaur National Monument has been eternally protected.

Who has protected you in challenging times? What cause or ideal deserves extra protection? What cause or ideal may not deserve the protection it once had?

Dinosaur National Monument's night sky is free from light pollution, making it an excellent site for stargazing.

WEIR FARM
NATIONAL HISTORIC SITE

CONNECTICUT • 1990 • EXPRESSION

*[God] has filled them with skill to do every kind of work done by an artisan or by
a designer or by an embroiderer in blue, purple, and crimson yarns, and in fine
linen, or by a weaver—by any sort of artisan or skilled designer.*
—Exodus 35:35 (NRSV)

"I don't know much about art, but I do know what I like when I see it!"
Stand near a painting in a museum and watch and listen to
people as they share their thoughts with one another. Each reaction is
as unique to them as the object they are viewing. Artists say that "Art is
what you bring to it," putting the burden of appreciation on the viewer.
Conventional wisdom says beauty is in the eye of the beholder. Tastes
and what is fashionable change. Works of art now viewed as masterpieces
and painters deemed to be "geniuses" were not always so well regarded
in their own times and places.

When the French painter Claude Monet put *Impression, soleil levant
[Impression, Sunrise]* on canvas in 1872, critics generally panned it. The
acceptable style in the art academies of Paris in Monet's time favored
works that hid all evidence of the painter's hand. The fashion was for
the image on the canvas to look as nearly realistic and lifelike as possible. Colors were muted, then varnished over to mute the light further
and hide traces of the brush. Monet and others like Renoir and Van
Gogh chose instead to focus on the play of light and its ever-changing
condition with their subject. They used brighter pastels, bolder colors,
and open, short brush strokes, with less focus on details via lines and
shading. Most of the impressionists painted outdoors and sought to
capture some element of the natural world.

Given how it was initially received, it is ironic that *Impression, Sunrise*

The Weir Farm on a rainy spring day

provided the appellation for an entire painting style. Monet, once widely criticized, is now considered a master, and his influence is far reaching.

Among those who followed Monet's style outside of France was American J. Alden Weir, considered to be among the greatest of the impressionists on this side of the pond. Weir Farm National Historic Site is one of only two sites in the National Park Service dedicated to the visual arts. Weir, his wife Anna, and their three daughters spent thirty-six years at the farm, acquired in a trade for a painting he owned plus ten dollars. Here you can walk the beautiful sixty acres of ground that inspired not only J. Alden but a host of North American artists. Thanks to the Art in the Park program, you can gaze upon the tree-lined pond or wander the pathways to capture an image that inspires you. You may even submit your work to the park to be considered in one of several juried categories that include junior, adult, and professional designations. Through an artist-in-residence program, you might be able to spend thirty days creating your own art in the Weir Studio. If you prefer to appreciate the work of others rather than create your own, there is a gallery to tour on the grounds.

The Weir Studio

Weir's *Black Hat* (oil on canvas)

In Exodus 35, people bring their items of value—gold, silver, brass, rare-colored threads, and other precious items—to be used in the building of the Tabernacle. Since this place would represent the dwelling place of God, the faithful were compelled to give the best they could offer. In addition, those who had artistic gifts used their talents to craft the items that would be used in the worship of God. Verse 35 refers to specific individuals whose talent was so spectacular, it was assumed their gifts must have come directly from God.

The artwork and the holy objects created for the Tabernacle attempted to embody the splendor and perfection of the Divine. The items themselves participated in transmitting the sacred nature of that which was beyond beauty and definition. From their very inception they represented the artist's love and devotion to Yahweh. All of the people in the community participated, either by giving their finest resources or contributing their best gifts. Such gifting of the self is reminiscent of Aristotle's thought that, "The aim of art is not to represent the outward appearance of things, but their inward significance."

What have you created, or offered resources for, that is an expression of inward significance in your life? What particular works of art convey meaning to you beyond their physical representation? How do you express your devotion to the Holy?

Weir's *The Veranda* (oil on canvas)

Old Swedes Church in Wilmington

FIRST STATE
NATIONAL HISTORICAL PARK

DELAWARE AND PENNSYLVANIA • 2015 • CONSENSUS

My dear friends, as a follower of our Lord Jesus Christ, I beg you to get along with each other. Don't take sides. Always try to agree in what you think.
—1 Corinthians 1:10 (CEV)

At one point in an American history class, your teacher summarized the different reasons each of the thirteen original colonies was established. The reason for Delaware's existence may have slipped your mind because of its diverse plethora of founders. A Dutch colony founded in 1631 lasted less than a year; seven years later and about eighty miles north, New Sweden was established by a group of Swedes, Finns, and Dutch before the English eventually gained control.

As the American Revolution neared, politically moderate Delaware lacked enthusiasm about splitting from Great Britain. When the Continental Congress met to debate the Declaration of Independence, Delaware's delegation nearly rejected the measure. John Dickinson epitomizes that middle-of-the-road outlook well. One of the colonies' wealthiest landowners, he was initially a Loyalist, supporting the monarch and believing the colonists' grievances lay with Parliament, not with King George. But he was also a proud colonist and apt to put his thoughts on paper, which earned him the nickname "Penman of the Revolution." He composed "The Liberty Song," which is among the first American patriotic songs; had King George heard it, he might have recognized that these colonists were no longer typical British subjects:

Come, join hand in hand, brave Americans all / And rouse
your bold hearts at fair Liberty's call; / No tyrannous acts
shall suppress your just claim / Or stain with dishonor America's name . . .

Then join hand in hand, brave Americans all, / By uniting we stand, by dividing we fall;

In so righteous a cause let us hope to succeed / For heaven approves of each generous deed.

In Freedom we're born and in Freedom we'll live. / Our purses are ready. Steady, friends, steady; / Not as slaves, but as Freemen our money we'll give.

Dickinson also helped write two statements that attempted to bridge the widening gap between the colonies and British rulers. Even though those petitions fell on deaf ears, Dickinson continued working toward reconciliation, refusing to vote for the Declaration of Independence as a delegate for Pennsylvania, where he also had a home. When the war started, he repeatedly declined leadership appointments to military posts, instead volunteering as needed.

John Dickinson

Despite his objections to independence and despite largely sitting out the war, Dickinson remained a respected statesman, and he helped draft the Articles of Confederation and later the Constitution. Dickinson, the only Founding Father to free his slaves between 1776 and 1786, argued vociferously against protecting slavery in the Constitution, but to no avail. Nevertheless, On December 7, 1787, Delaware's legislators approved the new Constitution, making Delaware the first of the thirteen colonies to act and giving it the eternal nickname "The First State."

Slave quarters at John Dickinson's plantation

It's a bit ironic that the First State was the last state to have a National Park Service unit, rectified by the creation of First State National Historical Park in 2015. Poplar House, Dickinson's house near the state capital of Dover, is one of several sites included in the park.

First State also memorializes those settlers who gave Delaware an early view of the diverse country America would become. Fort Christina, nestled in bustling Wilmington, was founded only after the native Leni Lenape sold the land to the arriving Swedes. Old Swedes Church hosts the country's oldest pulpit, dating back to 1698. Dover Green was the site of public readings of the Declaration of Independence, and the Constitution was ratified in a now-absent tavern off the green. To the north, the trails and streams of Beaver Valley offer hiking, biking, kayaking, and horseback riding. New Castle's courthouse hosted its share of historic events and trials and is a key geographic marker used to establish the state's unusual circular northern border. To the south, near the ill-fated Dutch colony, is the home of War of 1812 hero Jacob Jones.

When Dickinson died in 1808, Thomas Jefferson wrote, "a more estimable man, or truer patriot, could not have left us." Dickinson managed to work with those who disagreed with him, to find consensus, serving as many people as possible, as effectively as possible. He stood by his principles as circumstances changed, then adapted to the new circumstances.

When has consensus worked in your life? When has consensus back-fired for you? Do you wish you had chosen to seek consensus instead of standing by your own principles?

New Castle Court House Museum, New Castle

Footprints and tire tracks in the sand remind visitors of the same marks humans have left on the moon.

CANAVERAL NATIONAL SEASHORE

FLORIDA • 1975 • CONTRAST

Finally, brothers and sisters, whatever is true, whatever is noble,
whatever is right, whatever is pure, whatever is lovely, whatever is admirable—
if anything is excellent or praiseworthy—think about such things.
—PHILIPPIANS 4:8 (NIV)

Canaveral National Seashore is full of contrasts. Here the vast ocean ends and the land begins. Saltwater and freshwater mingle here. Heat-loving subtropical plants give way to hardier vegetation that can better weather the cold. Earth ends, and atmosphere begins, and above that, space. Here, the three environments that support life—water, earth, air—added a fourth, albeit within the protective confines of a spaceship.

When we hear the word *cañaveral* (Spanish for *reed bed* or *sugarcane plantation*), most of us think of space and rockets. Just across the bay, the Kennedy Space Center is where many of humanity's greatest voyages have begun. But some pretty incredible journeys begin on the sandy beaches too. From April to October, the beaches are nesting areas for four kinds of endangered sea turtles, including loggerhead and leatherbacks, Kemp's Ridley and green. An estimated twelve thousand known nests were identified in 2019, with each nest hosting about one hundred eggs. To emerge from these nests is a group effort for young turtles; the first hatchling waits until its siblings have hatched so they can, as a team, dig out of the sand and head for the ocean. Unlike the rockets propelling humans and cargo out of earth's gravity, the turtle hatchlings take it slow.

In all, the park hosts fifteen endangered species—including two snakes, five birds, manatees, the right whale, and a mouse. Those animals live among more than a thousand species of plants, and the different

The diverse lagoon ecosystem of Canaveral National Seashore

hot-and-cold plants coexist in the park. Three different types of mangrove provide habitat for the park's mobile residents: red mangroves live in the saltwater; black mangroves on the water's edge secrete salt through their leaves; and white mangroves in drier soil shed their salt through glands along the stems. Saw palmetto plays an important role in the ecosystem: kindling. Quite flammable, it fuels the fire that helps the ecosystem regenerate.

Like its better-known Florida siblings, Everglades and Biscayne national parks farther south, Canaveral National Seashore was born when residents recognized that the environment was disappearing beneath new air-conditioned cities. The barrier island and its bays were home to more than a thousand plants species, three hundred bird species, plus dolphins and manatees. A twenty-four-mile-long beach was still in pristine condition.

But many visitors to that beach aren't looking at the flora and fauna and water. They're looking into the distance. From Playalinda Beach, at the southern end of the park, it's only seven miles to Launch Pad 39A. Odds are you've seen that

NASA's launch facility can be seen from Playalinda Beach.

launch pad in film of the liftoffs of Apollo II and the space shuttles. Now NASA owns about two-thirds of the park and comanages it with the Merritt Island National Wildlife Refuge, under the administration of the US Fish and Wildlife Service. Together they partner on age-old problems like invasive species, land management, law enforcement, and mosquito control. They also work with park administrators to make launch days safe and enjoyable, when huge crowds can pack the park to capacity. How many National Park Service units close because of extraplanetary launches?

A space launch is surely a magnificent site, with fire and roaring and soaring. But after a few minutes, it's over, and we find ourselves still on the ground, awed by what we saw but perhaps grateful that we find ourselves in a nature preserve that shows us what the world has been like for thousands of years. And perhaps we'll be lucky enough to see a family of turtles beginning their own voyage.

It's no surprise that our faith gives us different ideas about to what we can compare and contrast different facets of our life. Scripture reminds us to avoid comparing because it causes envy or pride or other regrettable behaviors. Instead, scripture calls us to find contrasts within ourselves. God calls us to improve ourselves, and the only way we know how we're faring is to compare how we are now with how we were then. We grow, and we see the changes. Hopefully they're changes for the better; if they're not, our conscience may kick in and try to point us in the right direction.

Sea oats in sand dunes

What do you think are some of the more helpful comparisons you observe regularly? How are you working to improve yourself? How do you help others see the infinite possibilities before them?

MARTIN LUTHER KING JR. NATIONAL HISTORICAL PARK

GEORGIA • 2018 • HOPE

So the poor have hope, and injustice shuts its mouth.

—Job 5:16 (NIV)

Hope lingers in the dark night of winter, hidden deep in the soil where it cannot be seen but where its potential is undeniable.

Hope believes a different way of being exists despite all evidence to the contrary.

Hope stirs the smoldering ashes of courage into a raging conflagration of action.

Hope causes us to take a leap of faith when the ground below us eludes our eyes.

Hope bears the weight of the oppressor's yoke.

Hope sees a future reality that seems light years away as clearly as if it were in this present moment.

Where does hope come from? How does hope survive? How does hope yet to be realized not meld into bitterness? Scientists believe that hope is a mechanism in the brain that allows humans to adapt and survive in dangerous conditions. Not so Dr. Martin Luther King Jr. He believed that hope is grounded in the reality of God's desire for justice. Hope is not merely positive thinking, clever optimism, or wishing on a star. Justice, egalitarianism, and mercy—inherent characteristics of God—are immutable and set loose in the universe by the ubiquitous presence of the Divine, and therefore they cannot be resisted forever. Progress may be slow and setbacks common, however. "The moral arc of the universe is long, but it is bent toward justice," King said of the struggle for civil rights, paraphrasing the writing of nineteeenth-century Unitarian pastor Theodore Parker.

Martin Luther King Jr. birthplace on Auburn Avenue in Atlanta

The King Center, one of several places included in this National Historical Park, honors not just King's accomplishments but also the people who influenced him. Central in this list of philosophers, theologians, and activists is Mahatma Gandhi and his commitment to nonviolence. King blended the Gandhian pacifism of nonviolence with the Christian dictum to love *even the enemy*. He believed this was an unstoppable force. *"Darkness cannot drive out darkness—only light can do that."* The movement for civil rights had to be one of nonviolence because God abhorred killing, and history was littered with stories of the oppressed whose bonds, broken by force, simply became a new oppressor themselves.

Displays at King's birth home share that King was a typical child who didn't care much about practicing the piano. Yet the Ebenezer Baptist Church, where his father served as pastor before King Jr. was called to lead, demonstrates the pivotal role faith played in his life. From the pulpit, first father and then son proclaimed the First Testament prophets crying out for justice. Reading and studying texts from the perspective of the exploited gave credence to the idea that God is on the side of the oppressed and that liberation from bondage, breaking the yoke of injustice, is always God's preference.

Here King encountered and embraced the writings and teachings of great religious leaders and theologians such as Benjamin Mays, Walter Rauschenbusch, Howard Thurman, and Reinhold Niebuhr. The neighborhood itself reflects the old segregated

Ebenezer Baptist Church, where Martin Luther King and Martin Luther King Jr. served

South and its gradual transformation. In a park opposite Ebenezer Baptist Church is *Behold*, Patrick Morelli's sculpture depicting a man lifting a newborn child skyward. Morelli was inspired by the African tradition of lifting a child toward the heavens and reciting the words "Behold, the only thing greater than yourself." Nearby, the old fire

Inside the historic Ebenezer Baptist Church sanctuary

station #6, one of the first desegregated firehouses in Atlanta, served the Sweet Auburn community. The World Peace Garden is part of an international movement to teach peace and nonviolence to youth.

This National Historical Park is less about a place and more about how a man who grew up in this particular neighborhood became the very embodiment of hope as the most notable leader in the American civil rights movement. A reverent visit to the gravesite of Dr. and Mrs. King is a reminder of the price that is sometimes required of those who dare to dream that the way the world is, is not the way it has to be. King's wife, Coretta, and his family endured much suffering and loss as he struggled to be a voice in the halls of power for those who otherwise would not be heard. King himself paid for his dream with his own life.

For what do you hope? When has hope kept you going against all odds? How do you give others hope?

Tomb of Dr. and Mrs. King

Aerial view of the USS *Arizona* Memorial in Pearl Harbor

PEARL HARBOR
NATIONAL MEMORIAL

HAWAII • 1958 • SILENCE

And after the earthquake a fire, but the LORD was not in the fire;
and after the fire a sound of sheer silence.

—1 KINGS 19:12 (NRSV)

Quiet is the recognizable absence of noise. Silence is a moment waiting to be filled. Quiet occurs when the conductor steps to the podium, picks up the baton, and the stirring in the auditorium seats stills. Silence is what happens in between the moment the conductor's hand is raised and then starts to fall and the orchestra fills the hall with music.

Quiet is when you suddenly notice that the kids aren't making any sounds in the other room—and you are immediately alert! Silence is the wonder that overwhelms you at the sight of a child fast asleep. Silence permeates an occasion, and that silence may be filled with many things: wonder or amazement, anxiety or fear, joy or delight, sadness or grief—all of these can take up residence in silence. Whereas many of us seek after quiet, silence, by contrast, implies an encounter we cannot control. We do not sing "*Quiet* Night, Holy Night" in the candlelight of Christmas Eve, but rather "*Silent* Night, Holy Night."

When you take the short boat ride across Pearl Harbor to board the memorial that stretches across the shattered hull of the battleship USS *Arizona*, you can feel the distinct difference between quiet and silence. There is movement that gradually shifts everyone who visits from busy and distracted tourist, cameras at the ready, to intensely focused guest and discreet mourner. As the tiny watercraft that delivers you to the memorial finds its moorings and the dress-white uniformed pilot gives a solemn salute toward the American flag, there is only silence.

Any words now spoken are hushed whispers and respectful reflections.

It was fifteen minutes into the surprise attack on the quiet morning of December 7, 1941, that a bomb from a Japanese plane found its mark in the forward powder magazine of turret two and blew the ship apart. The ship sank forty feet to the bottom of the harbor as an estimated half of the one million gallons of Bunker C oil that turned her engines ignited in a great conflagration that burned for over two days. A thin ribbon of oil still escapes its holding tanks every day. Of the over 2,300 who lost their lives in the attack that day, 1,177 were listed as crew assigned to BB39, and over 900 are still entombed below deck under the tranquil waters.

When you stand on the memorial, you stand above a war grave. You are at the site where a second global war began. You feel the silence of a place made sacred not by the holy, but by the profane.

Sites on Battleship Row are managed by the United States Navy. Unlike the USS *Constitution* docked in Boston, the *Arizona* is no longer commissioned, but she does have the daily right to fly the country's colors as if still on active duty. Moored just a few yards from the *Arizona* is the USS *Missouri*. On that battleship's deck, forty-four months later, the Japanese surrendered to the Allies. The *Missouri* bookends World War II in a strikingly powerful pairing.

Respectful silence in the Shrine Room

It may strike you as ironic that Japanese visitors come to this shrine in equal or even greater numbers as people from the mainland. Here, people from the nation that eventually lost the war that began at this very site stand next to those whose country reeled from the strike and whose greatest generation ultimately prevailed.

And there is silence. In the silence, as you read the names of the dead engraved into the memorial, hangs remorse, disbelief, grief, anger, understanding, relief, resolution, and the nagging but rarely uttered question: "Why must we as a species continually go to war with one another?" Our human history has too many sites like this.

When Moses wanted to catch a glimpse of God, the Divine One wasn't in the wind, the earthquake, or the fire. God was in the holy silence. God filled the silence that, for a moment, Moses and the Divine shared. Moses

Flag at half-staff over the sunken battleship

was never the same. Is it any wonder that sometimes we want to avoid silence for fear of what might fill it?

When and why do you avoid silence? What fills the silence in your life? What would it mean for God to fill such a space?

One of the USS *Arizona* anchors displayed near the visitor's center

Indian Tunnel

CRATERS OF THE MOON NATIONAL MONUMENT AND PRESERVE

IDAHO • 1924 • AMAZEMENT

I saw a great many bones on the floor of the valley, bones that were very dry.
[The Lord] asked me, "Son of man, can these bones live?". . then [God] said to
me, "Prophesy to these bones and say to them, 'Dry bones, hear the word of the
Lord!'". . . So I prophesied as I was commanded. And as I was prophesying, there
was a noise, a rattling sound, and the bones came together, bone to bone. . . . And
a breath entered them; they came to life and stood up on their feet—a vast army.

—EZEKIEL 37:2, 3–4, 7, 10 (NIV)

As members of the only species to visit the moon, we know what its surface looks like from the photos we know so well: gray rock and gray powder, ridges on the horizon from craters that have never been eroded by wind or rain or glaciers, all the result of a long-ago ball of molten rock cooling in the vacuum of space. Desolate, empty, rugged, uninhabitable, and unforgiving, the moon is no place a human would want to stay very long, nor could we without bringing along every single thing we need to survive. It's a miracle that humanity made it to the moon and back all those times without a single fatality.

Craters of the Moon National Monument and Preserve earned its name long before humanity got an up-close look at the lunar surface, but the comparison is easy to see. Thirty million years of geologic activity have pushed mountains higher and valleys lower, with volcanoes punching through the cracks. This stark landscape has formed in the last fifteen thousand years, with the most recent flow only two thousand years old. The park includes about sixty lava flows and twenty-five volcanic cones, plus caves and lava tubes for adventurers seeking a little subterranean darkness.

Different lavas at Craters of the Moon National Monument: Ropy pahoehoe, Blue Dragon, and Breadcrust

To the untrained eye, lava is merely melted rock, but Craters of the Moon has several different kinds of lava. *Block lava* created a surface of angular blocks. Áa lava created a rough, spiky surface. Smooth *pahoehoe* lava came in three varieties: *slabby*, which is jumbled plates or slabs of broken pahoehoe crust; *shelly*, laced with small tubes, bubbles, and thin crusts; and *spiny*, containing gas bubbles that form spines.

These different kinds of lava are each created in unique ways, and to scientists who study the history of the earth and our solar system, those differences matter. That's one reason that in 1969, four NASA astronauts visited the park for a crash course on volcanic geology, preparation for what they hoped would be useful knowledge 239,000 miles overhead on the lunar surface. The neophyte geologists learned how to spot igneous rocks that would provide the best study subjects back on earth. Three of those astronauts ended up leaving their bootprints in the moon-dust and brought back samples that are still studied today.

The six hundred-plus square miles of Craters of the Moon National Monument is not a solid lava field. Dotted throughout the park are more

Volcanic bombs ejected years ago

than five hundred *kipukas*, elevated patches of older lava that stayed above more recent lava flows. Islands of life, kipukas that have collected enough soil and vegetation are easy to spot in the park's barren expanses, and they support the ecosystem's tough permanent residents. Tucked among the sagebrush and grasses and Idaho's oldest juniper trees dwell 58 species of mammals, 212 species of birds, ten of reptiles, and four amphibian species. In a once-lifeless place, there is again life—a miracle like Ezekiel's legion of dry bones.

Pahoehoe lava and North Crater

Since we first looked starward and realized we could see more than pinpricks of light, the moon has inspired humanity's spiritual and philosophical reflections. Humanity's visit to the moon may have changed how we envision that layered understanding of "what lies beyond"— heaven above, hell below, our lives in the middle where we individually determine our soul's ultimate destination. You and I may not get to experience the miracle of interplanetary travel, but we can marvel at the miracles humanity may yet achieve. Craters of the Moon is a place where we can perceive the simultaneous progress of both technology and religion.

What is the most amazing accomplishment you have ever seen or heard of? What have you done that makes you wonder even now, *How did I pull that off?* What is something you hope to achieve in your life that seems just shy of impossible?

Apollo 14 astronauts Alan Shepard, Gene Cernan, Ed Mitchell, and backup Joe Engle during their 1969 training

PULLMAN NATIONAL MONUMENT

ILLINOIS • 2015 • LABOR

*For the scripture says "You shall not muzzle an ox while it is treading out
the grain," and, "The laborer deserves to be paid."*
—1 TIMOTHY 5:18 (NRSV)

Begun in 1867, the Pullman Palace Car Company was synonymous
with luxury train travel. George Pullman made his fortune working for the city of Chicago as it added sanitation services. During this
experience, he spent a great deal of time on trains between Chicago and
his home in New York. He found the railcars—especially the sleeping
cars—to be uncomfortable. Necessity being the mother of invention,
Pullman designed a high-quality sleeping railcar and built thousands
of them at a plant outside of Chicago.

Pullman believed in improving the lives of his workers. New manufacturing methods required a better workforce, providing him with an
opportunity to try something new: a planned industrial community.
On four thousand acres, Pullman built houses and created what was to
become the first American "company" town. Adjacent to the factory,
and with indoor plumbing and alleyways for trash collection, it was
intended both to be convenient and to establish a higher standard of
living. Rent was automatically deducted from each worker's paycheck.

A financial panic in 1893 slowed demand for the passenger cars,
and salaries of the workforce were cut—yet the rent charged for compa-
ny-owned housing and dividends paid to stockholders remained the
same. By 1894, worker discontent boiled over, and a strike was called.
With the Pullman company in a financial position to withstand the
stoppage, the American Railway Union added pressure by insisting its
members not run trains with Pullman cars. The ubiquitous nature of
Pullman cars across the country meant that this boycott crippled the

Row houses from the original Pullman company town

The Pullman Porter was a sign of luxury and hospitality.

Living conditions for workers during the 1894 strike

national railway system. In an attempt to break the strike, the company worked to have their passenger cars hitched to mail cars, which in turn would disrupt mail delivery and turn public sentiment away from support of the boycott and the disgruntled workers.

What happened instead was that federal government intervened to end the boycott under the Sherman Anti-Trust Law of 1890. Federal troops were called in to Pullman, where violence ensued, and many lives were lost—as was the cause of the workers. This event spurred the establishment of the federal government's authority to involve itself in securing the free flow of interstate commerce. Following investigations into what had transpired during the strike, the Illinois Supreme Court ordered the Pullman company to divest itself of its ownership of the "company town." George Pullman's reputation was so damaged, the vitriol was so great, that he ordered his grave to be covered with tons of steel and concrete to protect his body from desecration.

Robert Todd Lincoln, son of the great president, became the next president of the Pullman company, and he revived the company's reputation and increased the quality of the railcars by moving to all-steel construction in 1908. This retooling meant new jobs.

But labor unrest would again visit the company. One aspect that improved the reputation of Pullman railcars was the service provided by the Pullman Porters, primarily African American men trained to provide excellent service to rail passengers. Pullman Porters enjoyed a unique status within the black community even though they worked for little better than slave wages and tips. They formed the Brotherhood of Sleeping Car Porters or BSCP, and in 1937, under the leadership of A. Phillip Randolph, BSCP signed an agreement with the Pullman company for better wages and working conditions for the people who made up nearly 40 percent of its workforce. In a country gripped with racism and divided by socioeconomic classism, this acquiescence to the black union's demands was groundbreaking and important for raising the status of all black workers. The BSCP remained a civil rights organization throughout the 1960s, seeking justice and fair wages for working women and men of color. A museum dedicated to the BSCP and Randolph is a part of the Pullman National Monument.

The restored administration building

Justice for the worker is a deeply rooted theme in the biblical witness. God demands fairness for those who labor and a reward for those who produce for the common good. It is expected that the employer will provide a fair wage and will be held accountable by the Divine if they fail to do so. That high standard is meant to reflect a generous God.

Do you believe in a fair wage for all workers? How are we to determine what is economically just? When workers depend on tips for service, how generous are you?

Pullman sleeping car circa 1950

LINCOLN BOYHOOD NATIONAL MEMORIAL

INDIANA • 1960 • ORIGINS

Eliud the father of Eleazar, and Eleazar the father of Matthan, and Matthan
the father of Jacob, and Jacob the father of Joseph the husband of Mary,
of whom Jesus was born, who is called the Messiah.

—MATTHEW 1:15–16 (NRSV)

Indiana is the Hoosier state, an appellation proudly taken by the majority of its residents and as the nickname for its largest public university's sports teams. However, ask anyone in Indiana what a Hoosier is and no one can give you a definitive answer. The etiology of the word is imprecise at best. Some will say that the name developed around a contractor working in Indiana whose name was Hoosier. He employed a large workforce, which became known as Hoosier's men. Others will say the name is a derivative of "Who's here?" as people might ask in calling out into the woods or in answering a knock at the door, requesting that strangers identify themselves. Another theory posits that its origin is from the Native American word *hoosa*, which means corn. A favorite explanation among the populace in the southern portion of the state is that it came from "Who's your," as in "Who's your daddy?"

The latter question, though more likely a modern idiom, may still have some credence, as people are often identified by their lineage and familial connections. "Who's your people?" may be a closer approximation, for settlers encountering one another wanted a way to identify possible connections to new neighbors. As land opened up in the Northwest Territory, people traveled from other regions to seek their fortunes or to get a fresh start.

Such was the case of Thomas and Nancy Lincoln, who moved their young family, including seven-year-old Abraham, to Indiana from

Boyhood home of Abraham Lincoln

Sculpted panel representing Lincoln's time in Indiana, by E. H. Daniels

Sinking Springs, Kentucky, in 1816. There, issues with faulty land titles cost the Lincolns their farm, and they chose to head north to a free state. They established a farm outside of Little Pigeon Creek Community, Indiana, named for the immense population of passenger pigeons that were said to darken a noonday sky when they took flight.

It is here, proclaim modern-day Hoosiers with pride, that the sixteenth president grew up and was shaped by "Hoosier" values during the most formative years of his life. These are the people who influenced him and prepared him for leadership in what would become the most critical time in the nation's history. Honesty, integrity, a love for learning, genuine compassion for others, and his moral compass all came from his time in Indiana and the people with whom he associated. These people and this environment were the origins of what made Abraham Lincoln who he was.

A trip to Lincoln's childhood home is a glimpse into the world where the hardships and prosperity of life on the frontier can be viewed

Period reenactments are a feature of this historic park.

through the recreated cabin where Abe and his stepbrothers slept in the loft of the single-room dwelling. This is where he grieved his mother's death, learned the reward of hard work, honed his skills with an axe, and received the education that led to the eloquence of the Gettysburg Address and the principled conviction of the Emancipation Proclamation.

The memorial building on the grounds displays five sculpted panels created by E. H. Daniels that portray five key periods of Lincoln's life, one being his time in this place in southern Indiana. The beautiful grounds at the memorial, including the walkway to Nancy Hanks Lincoln's gravesite, were designed by landscape architect Frederick Law Olmsted Jr., and include a 120-foot flagpole, the tallest in the National Park Service.

A debate in social sciences and psychology has raged for years about what shapes humans into who we are as individuals. Is it genetics or environment—nature or nurture? Ongoing studies with twins over half a century suggest it is both. Who our people are in terms of genetics certainly plays a role. Environment and life events also have a significant impact. We generally skip over the biblical "begats" and the long list of hard-to-pronounce names when reading Scripture. Yet the authors listed these heirs to show the connections and origins of the people featured in the stories, which in turn placed them in the context of history, to demonstrate they didn't just appear out of nowhere. They had roots and stories that formed and influenced them.

How does your family of origin shape who you have become? What do you know about your ancestry? Which do you suppose has had more influence on you, your genetics or your environment?

Trail of twelve stones, containing stones from major events in Lincoln's life

Marching Bear Mounds in summertime splendor

EFFIGY MOUNDS
NATIONAL MONUMENT

IOWA • 1949 • DOMINION

Then God said, "Let us make man in our image, after our likeness.
And let them have dominion over the fish of the sea and over the birds of the
heavens and over the livestock and over all the earth and over
every creeping thing that creeps on the earth."
—GENESIS 1:26 (ESV)

Animal names are among the first words humans learn. Cartoon images of the animals and their sounds—*moo, quack, neigh, baa*—are staples of learning to communicate about the world around us. A trip to the zoo or aquarium is a favorite for people of many ages. We observe the animals and their quirks, and learn about their foods and their habitats. Fishing lets us glimpse into the wet world, briefly bringing a trout out of the water and then, if the trout is lucky, releasing it back into the stream.

When we buy processed food from the grocery stores and clothes made from blends of plants and chemicals, it's easy to feel disconnected from nature. But there are places we can visit to reconnect with the role that our world's co-inhabitants play in our lives.

On the riverbanks overlooking the upper Mississippi River valley is Effigy Mounds National Monument, a legacy of Native Americans acknowledging the nature around them. In past centuries, mounds like these could be found in Wisconsin, Minnesota, Illinois, and Iowa, many dating back to around the same era, between 800 to 1,350 years ago, when these mounds were built. They represented a North American zoo: birds, bears, deer, snakes, bison, turtles, panthers, turtles— and waters.

At the monument, more than two hundred such mounds, including three dozen effigies, have been protected. These are not towering

Hanging Rock and the Mississippi River

markers by any means; they're fairly low-profile, like the undulations of a golf course, maybe three feet tall. It would be easy to overlook them—until you take the time to notice the not-so-random shapes of the mounds. Effigy Mounds is full of birds and bears. At the southern end of the park, Marching Bear Group contains ten bears and a trio of birds. Farther north is Great Bear Mound, more than 135 feet across.

Who created these mounds is lost to history, but twenty Native American tribes trace their lineage back to the mound builders. Being on high ground, the mounds may have been visible from a distance. Some are burial mounds, but what about the others? Archaeological evidence is ambiguous, and protective legislation prevents even the best-intentioned researcher from significantly altering the mounds. The hunch is that the mounds marked good locations to find food, sacred sites, celestial markers, or territorial boundaries.

Effigy Mounds is more than the mounds, though. It's unique in its location in the Midwest, on the banks of the great American river. Perched atop bluffs soaring hundreds of feet above the Mississippi River, its trails provide breathtaking views of an area once considered for national park status. Tallgrass prairies, largely eradicated by grazing and farming, are taking root once again in the rich Iowa soil. The park abuts a 261-mile-long wildlife refuge and a state park, expanding the protected area. The animals that inspired the effigies may be rare nowadays, but plenty of animals still call the area home.

The United States has set aside vast tracts of land for animals; nearly a million square miles of land and water are protected by federal law. A variety of government agencies at the federal, state, county, and local levels manage these sites and protect the natural habitats of countless animals and plants. Politics rarely divides us on this directive;

An aerial view of the Marching Bear Mounds

three-quarters of Americans surveyed believe the United States should do whatever it takes to protect the environment. In the place we occupy as the most intelligent animals on the planet, we have an obligation to the animals and plants and all the living creatures—not just to care *about* them but to care *for* them. That means more than feeding the dog, cleaning the aquarium, or watering the flowers. We are called to keep the air and water clean and the forests and grasses healthy. We have a duty to leave the world in better shape than we found it. We can use nature, of course, but we must take care of it responsibly.

What do you do already to care for animals and plants? What can you do to be a better environmental caretaker? How does your faith influence how you view the environment?

Autumn at Fire Point

NICODEMUS
NATIONAL HISTORIC SITE

When Pharaoh let the people go, God didn't lead them by way of the land
of the Philistines, even though that was the shorter route. God thought,
If the people have to fight and face war, they will run back to Egypt.
So God led the people by the roundabout way of the Reed Sea desert.
—EXODUS 13:17–18 (CEB)

Staying in your home is no longer an option for you and your children, surrounded by violence, hatred, oppression, and no chance
of change. Leaving is your only choice for your survival, and even that
isn't guaranteed. You might die on the way to safety. You might arrive
in the promised land only to find you are unwelcome, unable to stay,
and you must move on, or maybe go back to where you came from. But
going is clearly the better choice than staying, even if it means dying
far from home.

It's a familiar conundrum these days as people all over the world flee
violence, oppression, the effects of climate change, and famine. After
the Civil War in the United States, former slaves—legally emancipated
but still enslaved by the economy and prejudice—wondered if they could
truly be free anywhere. Some cast their eyes west, to the still-sparsely
populated Great Plains.

One group of settlers with the goal of establishing the first all-black
settlement on the Great Plains believed their new home would be
Nicodemus, Kansas. In April 1877, less than a week before Reconstruction formally ended in the South, seven Kansans (six black and
one white) found a potential town site on the banks of the Solomon
River in the state's northwestern quadrant. What inspired Nicodemus's
naming is still debated. The National Park Service says the song "Wake

District #1 schoolhouse, built in the early 1900s

Nicodemus," which encouraged blacks to migrate, was the inspiration. Others offer Nicodemus, a Pharisee who helped entomb Jesus after the Crucifixion, as the source, a leader whose life Jesus changed. Certainly the future residents of Nicodemus were ready for their lives to change.

Settlers from eastern Kansas and Kentucky began arriving that June, unprepared for the new setting. Lacking tools needed to farm the drier terrain and too poor to purchase those supplies, they built homes of prairie sod and scraped the soil with handheld tools. Charities, other communities, and even the Osage tribe provided initial support.

After two years, wealthier settlers from Kentucky and Mississippi brought horses and equipment so desperately needed to keep the colony alive, but their arrival affected the social dynamic too. With Nicodemus finally showing signs of growth, the town's new leading class rejected others' charity in the hopes of discouraging Exodusters, poor slaves following the Mississippi River north and hoping to find their own opportunities in Kansas.

For a while, Nicodemus was a going concern. Notoriously inconsistent census reports show the town had 358 residents, three-quarters of whom were black; several hundred more black residents lived elsewhere in the county, about 20 percent of the county's population. Among the thirty-five structures recorded in 1881 were three hotels, two livery stables, two churches, stores, and other businesses. Nicodemus was in the running to be named the Graham County

The Nicodemus Buffalo Soldiers Association's performace is a highlight of the annual Emancipation Celebration.

seat. (The victor in the election was Millbrook, wiped off the map by a tornado less than a decade later.)

Eventually, though, fortunes changed. The local economy soured, and residents left. An error filing the ownership deed threw the town's future into doubt. Railroads bypassed Nicodemus, and the town faced the same fate of so many tiny Great Plains communities.

Nicodemus African Methodist Episcopal church

Nicodemus still had its share of supporters; annual emancipation celebrations drew thousands in the 1920s, and reunions continued for decades. But as the post-war American suburbs boomed, Nicodemus lost first its post office and then its school.

New life stirred in the 1970s, and in 1996, Nicodemus National Historic Site was created to preserve this remarkable town and to honor its visionaries. The park has five buildings—the township hall, the schoolhouse, the St. Francis Hotel and Switzer Residence, the Old First Baptist Church (still an active congregation), and the African Methodist Episcopal (A.M.E.) Church—two of which are open to the public.

Nicodemus lies below the eternal Kansas skies, a promised land for some, just another unwelcoming place for others. For all who made the trek, though, it represented the hope of a new place and a new life.

When in your life have you needed to start over? When did you need to risk everything in hopes of a better day? How have you helped somebody else in that situation?

An autumn sunset

Poor Valley Ridge and Cumberland Mountain in winter

CUMBERLAND GAP
NATIONAL HISTORICAL PARK

KENTUCKY, TENNESSEE, AND
VIRGINIA • 1959 • PATHWAY

Make me to know your ways, O LORD; teach me your paths.

—PSALM 25:4 (NRSV)

Geographically speaking, the Appalachian Mountains stretch from the Canadian island of Newfoundland to central Alabama. Geologically speaking, they are older than the Rockies and the Alps and stood equally tall in their "youth." Sociologically speaking, these mountains have often isolated the people who call them home because of the difficulty in traversing them. This has remained true into the twenty-first century due to the logistics and the expense of delivering everything from modern utility services to groceries being higher there than in other parts of the country.

The Appalachians posed significant challenges to westward expansion in the United States. Steep cliffs and enclosed deep valleys made travel by land so challenging that most of the population, even late into the 1700s, lived east of the range back toward the Atlantic seaboard. The natural gap within the Cumberland Mountains, believed to be the remnant of a meteor impact 300 million years ago, was "discovered" in 1750 by Judge Thomas Walker. Prior to his encounter with this natural passage, though, the gap had been used by buffalo, elk, and other wildlife as well as the Shawnee, Cherokee, and the Yuchi native people.

In 1775, Richard Henderson wanted to build a colony named Transylvania west of the mountains. He hired Daniel Boone to create and mark a path through the gap. Boone's adventures made him an American legend. His exploits of being captured by Native Americans, escaping, and being captured again became lore in both the

Cumberland Gap passage is not only used by humans.

United States and England. The story goes that during one of his captivities he learned of a pending surprise attack upon Fort Boonsboro, the colony Boone had established. He escaped and traveled 160 miles in four days across unforgiving land to alert the fort's inhabitants. Forewarned and prepared, they thwarted the attack and forced a Shawnee retreat.

It took Boone and thirty axmen two weeks to clear and mark the passage into eastern Kentucky, and it was a game changer to the growth of the young nation. By the early 1820s more than one hundred thousand people had traveled the "wilderness road" and walked through the Cumberland Gap to seek their fortune in the newly accessible West. The National Park Service estimates that today, forty-seven million Americans are the descendants of these westward venturing pioneers.

During the Civil War, Lincoln wanted the gap and high ground around it for the Union troops to choke Confederate supply routes and as a means to take eastern Tennessee. Rebel forces captured and used the gap for an incursion into Kentucky. No major battles were fought here, but it remained

Cumberland Gap from White Rocks

strategically important throughout the war and changed hands several times. Remnants of gabions—fortifications and barriers built into the mountain by both sides—remain for curious tourists to admire.

Though the gap no longer serves as a passage to the West, a tunnel now connects Middleboro, Kentucky, to Cumberland Gap, Tennessee, making travel easier. The park provides for hiking and camping, giving those venturing through it breathtaking vistas encompassing three states. Within its boundaries are 970 species of vascular plants, 90 of which are classified as sensitive or rare. Twenty-seven species of fish swim in its streams, and 147 species of birds call the park home for all or part of the year. Twenty-four cave features, ranging from twenty feet to sixteen miles in length, are a part of the park.

While passing through the gap is done on ground that is anything but flat, it is an easier pathway than either a direct vertical assault on the neighboring mountains or meandering miles in the opposite direction through the nearby valleys. The Bible asserts that to know God and have the desire to serve God by living in the world on God's terms, is in essence a pathway—a safe passage to a better and more fulfilling way of living. When one stays on the path, one is not nearly as likely to get lost.

Reenactment of pioneers crossing through the Gap

What pathways have you discovered that make life easier? When was a time you were lost and off the pathway? How did you find your way back?

NEW ORLEANS JAZZ
NATIONAL HISTORICAL PARK

LOUISIANA • 1994 • MUSIC

David and all the Israelites were celebrating with all their might before God,
with songs and with harps, lyres, timbrels, cymbals and trumpets.
—1 CHRONICLES 13:8 (NIV)

Perhaps no city in the world is more closely linked with a particular style of music than New Orleans is with jazz. If you visit New Orleans and don't see a busking musician on a street corner, perhaps you need to venture beyond your hotel room. Jazz was born in New Orleans, and ever since the musical style has influenced American music of all kinds—blues, rock and roll, classical, gospel, and hip-hop.

New Orleans epitomizes the American convergence and interplay of cultures that defines America. Native Americans interacted with the French settlers who founded New Orleans along the unexplored Mississippi River. The Louisiana Purchase and the War of 1812 cemented America's hold on the region, and New Orleans became the third-largest American city and was the South's largest city for nearly a century. African American culture added to the milieu, creating a city that at the beginning of the twentieth century produced the quintessential American musical genre.

Start with a steady rhythm. Add brass, woodwinds, and piano. When appropriate, sing. Then add creativity, improvisation, and syncopation. That's jazz, at least in its roots. Over a century, jazz has evolved into many different strains, from the simple piano player in a club to hundreds of musicians playing American standards during college football halftimes. Jazz is everywhere, all the time.

Today, we can visit jazz's birthplace at New Orleans Jazz National Historic Park, across Rampart Street from the legendary French

Brass band at Chalmette Battlefield

New Orleans Jazz National Historic Park is one of the few places you may see a sousaphone on the sidewalk.

Quarter. It makes sense that the park is centered on Louis Armstrong Park, named for the New Orleans native and jazz's first superstar. Preservation Hall, the heart of the Louis Armstrong Park, was a Masonic lodge that hosted social events, one of the places where segregated New Orleanians crossed their own racial lines. At just four acres, the park serves as the focal point for an exploration into the neighboring areas to see the legendary venues where jazz entered our culture.

Many of jazz's historical landmarks have been torn down by urban "progress" like highways, stadiums, and housing projects, but the neighborhoods still exist. Each of those neighborhoods—Tango Belt, Tremé, Back o' Town, South Rampart, the 6th, 7th, 8th , and 9th Wards, and the Pontchartrain lakefront—lay claim to their own musicians with their own visions of what jazz could be. Best known (or, perhaps, infamous) may be Storyville, the seedy neighborhood that was a legal red-light district for two decades, the same era when jazz arose. Little of Storyville remains now, but the more adventurous can take walking or driving tours to pay homage to the plot of ground where musical creativity reigned. If you're lucky,

Mardi Gras spirit

you might get to join a jazz parade through those same neighborhoods.

In the heart of the French Quarter is Preservation Hall. Founded in the 1950s as an art museum that hosted musicians, the performers proved a more popular draw, and the building became a concert venue. Today Preservation Hall hosts multiple concerts each night and welcomes all ages so that young musicians can sample the fun, creative music while they're still developing their own musical tastes. How many National Park Service units have musicians as park rangers?

When jazz was born, its melodies went only as far as the muggy bayou air would allow. Then radio and movies, then television, the Internet, and portable music players have made it possible for us to hear music from around the world. You can hear the same musicians playing on radio stations in Indianapolis or Istanbul. The amazing diversity in the music we hear plays to our emotions, draws out our memories, and inspires our own creativity. Sacred music draws us back to the roots of our faith and reminds us of the holy in our lives. Contemporary worship music updates those themes and fuses them with the music we hear each day, an acknowledgment that our faith, our world, and our very selves are changing all the time. We have moments every day to improvise, to find ways to syncopate our own rhythms, change things up, and create something we've never heard before.

What music most deeply resonates with you and helps you see things differently? When has music inspired you do to something courageous or bold? How do you make your own music?

You're never too young or too old to learn a new instrument!

View from the Appalachian Trail's northern
end point (or start point) at Mount Katahdin

APPALACHIAN NATIONAL SCENIC TRAIL

MAINE • 1937 • PREPARATION

A voice cries out: "In the wilderness prepare the way of the LORD,
make straight in the desert a highway for our God."

—ISAIAH 40:3 (NRSV)

Though it traverses fourteen states, the Appalachian National Scenic Trail either begins or ends 5,267 feet above sea level on the Maine summit of Mount Katahdin, 2,190 miles northeast of Springer Mountain, Georgia. Along that route, it traces the spine of the eastern mountain range that shares the trail's name.

The through-hike rises and falls an estimated total of 515,000 feet in elevation, enough to equal the climb up to the summit of Mount Everest over seventeen times. For the average hiker, it will take six months to complete and travel through the most biologically diverse area of all of the National Park Service units. It traverses remote regions east of the Mississippi, and yet also comes surprisingly close to many major cities. Not only will you have to learn how to watch your footing along a rocky ridgeline with steep drop-offs on your right and left, you'll also figure out how to cross a major highway with all of your gear intact.

Under the stewardship of the National Park Service, the trail represents a unique partnership between the government and dozens of local volunteer organizations that take responsibility for the path's maintenance and work for its continued preservation and protection. Local clubs clear overgrown brush, repair washouts, build crossings over streams and gullies, and keep the bright yellow "AT" blazes visible to guide those sojourning the pathway. They also advocate to keep encroaching development from destroying this undisturbed

The Appalachian Trail crosses remote and populated areas. This blaze can be found in Hot Springs, North Carolina.

wilderness. A great deal of preparation goes into making the trail ready for those who accept the challenge to traverse its course.

Getting the trail prepared for hikers is one thing. Getting hikers prepared for the trail is another! Those who embark on the trek without training for the journey rarely survive the first two weeks. Advice is ubiquitous: exercise is essential. Walk, bike, run, swim, and do it with an eye toward building endurance. But exercise is not enough. You need to seek out similar terrain to what you will experience on the trail and you need to walk with your pack—in the rain, the cold, and the heat, because that is what you will encounter day after day after day.

Every expert agrees you need to test your equipment and know how to use it *before* you go. Break in your boots or shoes—and don't skimp to save money on this essential part or your gear. Honest experts also share that there are certain "necessities" you need to practice as well, for instance—how shall we say this delicately?—to do in the woods what bears do in the woods.

Aside from learning how to sleep on the ground, in a tent, in the woods, you also need to prepare for very close encounters with

Appalachian Trail atop Loft Mountain

nature. Bugs and bears are the obvious concerns, and you must be ready to contend with both. On the bonus side you will get to see birds, wildflowers, and small mammals across an incredibly diverse set of biozones. On the section of trail that traverses Great Smoky Mountain National Park, you will cross over Clingman's Dome and catch a view from 6,625 feet of elevation, a sight you will have the satisfaction of knowing you have earned with every step up the mountain.

Whether you attempt a through-hike or just a section at a time, the Appalachian Trail provides the ready and willing with a test of self as well as a front-seat view to the majestic and subtle beauty that makes up the eastern United States. The better prepared you are, the more enjoyable the trip will be—which, perhaps, is not unlike the walk of faith. Faith is best practiced in a community that has prepared our pathway with the knowledge of tradition and wisdom of experience so as to assure us we can find secure footing and honest direction. When lived in the discipline of discipleship—through study, worship, service, prayer, and the practice of generosity, we grow stronger and are better able to meet the challenges our belief demands. It's all about the preparation.

How do you prepare for a challenge? When has preparation made a notable difference in your life? How might you share your experience to help others prepare?

The trail from Georgia to Maine

HARRIET TUBMAN UNDERGROUND RAILROAD NATIONAL HISTORICAL PARK

MARYLAND • 2013 • RISK

Moses and Aaron went to Pharaoh and said, "This is what the Lord,
Israel's God, says: 'Let my people go so that they can hold a festival for me in the
desert.'" But Pharaoh said, "Who is this Lord whom I'm supposed to obey by
letting Israel go? I don't know this Lord, and I certainly won't let Israel go."
—Exodus 5:1–2 (CEB)

The pre-Civil War era is the darkest time of American history. Slavery shadows all of American history, a shadow that hasn't fully vanished as America struggles to shake loose of a long history of persecution and subjugation of African Americans.

The abolitionist heroes of those days are legends: lawmakers in the halls of Congress, pastors in the pulpits, soldiers on the battlefields, women who courageously lectured and created antislavery literature, but especially those who created the Underground Railroad. Of those legends, Harriet Tubman stands above them all for her powerful story and what she accomplished against all the odds.

The woman who would become Harriet Tubman was born in 1822 as Araminta Ross, a slave in eastern Maryland. One of nine children, Tubman was separated from her father at a very young age, and three sisters were sold to another slaveowner in the Deep South. As a six-year-old, Tubman was rented out to other slaveowners to catch muskrats in the swamps along Chesapeake Bay. In so doing, she learned the lay of the land and befriended neighbors and sailors passing by on the bay. She built a network that would serve her well in the coming years.

Eventually Tubman married a freeman and took her mother's first name, Harriet. In 1849, Tubman's owner died, increasing the odds

Harriet Tubman shepherded escaping slaves through Eastern Shore wetlands like these.

she could be sold to a far-off slaveowner and even harsher conditions. Traveling by night in the marsh's protective cover and using the contacts she'd made, Tubman fled north to Pennsylvania. "When I found I had crossed that line, I looked at my hands to see if I was the same person," she later said. "There was such a glory over everything; the sun came like gold through the trees, and over the fields, and I felt like I was in Heaven." There she met abolitionists and became a nationally sought speaker and organizer. She also hatched a plan to put her life of slavery to use freeing others.

Beginning the following year, Tubman began venturing back to Maryland to assist fleeing slaves—a movement that became known as the Underground Railroad. Across the country, an estimated hundred thousand people were freed thanks in part to the Underground Railroad; about seventy people found freedom thanks to Tubman herself plus another seventy she assisted along the way.

A woman of deep faith who professed she had divine visions, Tubman sang two songs as she worked, "Go Down Moses" and "Bound for the Promised Land," that both inspired her and, depending on the tempo at which she sang, served as a signal to those she worked to free. Imagine the battling emotions of hope and terror when she started singing!

Malone Methodist Episcopal church, founded in 1864

Tubman served a stint during the Civil War in South Carolina leading Union forces in an operation that resulted in the freeing of more than 750 slaves. Following the war, she and her second husband adopted a baby girl and moved to Auburn, New York; her home there is the Harriett Tubman National Historic Park, a sister NPS unit. Until her death in 1913, she was a noted activist supporting equal treatment not only of African Americans but also of all women.

The Harriet Tubman Underground Railroad National Historic Park in the Delmarva Peninsula preserves the environment where Tubman grew up and learned her skills. The plantation where she grew up is in the park, and a wildlife preserve gives visitors the opportunity to see a world of safe shelters and bewildering wilderness that helped Tubman hide her charges. The home of Jacob Jackson, who relayed a message from Tubman to her brothers that help was on the way, is a centerpiece for the park. Other historic buildings empower visitors to imagine the community that produced this remarkable woman.

Harriet Tubman, circa 1868, from an album unveiled in 2019

Had she been captured, Tubman surely would have paid the ultimate price for her work, and history would now be remembering her as a martyr. Instead, we remember her for her bravery, ingenuity, and compassion. She put everything she had on the line so others could be free.

What is the most you've ever put on the line for others? How do you determine just how committed you are to a cause? Whom do you know who has been willing to sacrifice the way Tubman did?

At this Bucktown store or one nearby, Harriet Tubman sustained a head injury when she refused to help an overseer capture an escaping slave.

"Fairsted," the Olmsted home and studio as seen from a lower garden

FREDERICK LAW OLMSTED NATIONAL HISTORIC SITE

MASSACHUSETTS • 1979 • DESIGN

The heavens are telling the glory of God;
and the firmament proclaims his handiwork.
—Psalm 19:1 (NRSV)

Visit a park in most any modestly sized city in the United States and you are probably standing in a space designed by or inspired by Frederick Law Olmsted. His firm was responsible for over six thousand landscape commissions in forty-six states. He is the father of American landscape architecture, and from New York City's Central Park to Piedmont Avenue in Berkeley, California, his legacy of creating pastoral settings amid metropolitan areas is a gift of tranquility to millions of visitors. The grounds of the United States Capitol, the greenway beside Niagara Falls' rushing waters, Prospect Park in Brooklyn, the Biltmore Estate in North Carolina, several universities, and other spaces we know by sight had their natural beauty drawn out on the drafting board in his studio. The National Historic Site preserves "Fairsted," his home and office in the Boston suburb of Brookline, where his eye for nature's loveliness empowers us to discover for ourselves the wonder in the landscape before us—by design.

Olmsted had no formal education beyond the age of fourteen. He apprenticed as a clerk in a dry goods import business, served as crewman on a merchant ship to China, owned a farm for a time, and took a walking tour of Europe. His first book was on his experience as an American farmer visiting Europe; another series of books, written at the invitation of the editor of the *New York Daily Times*, scrutinized the social impact of slavery in the South. Later, while working for the Mariposa Gold Mining Company in California, he wrote about conservation,

Frederick Law Olmsted's drafting table, where many park designs were created

A ranger leads a program for children on the Fairsted grounds.

inspired by his visit to the nearby Yosemite Valley. This particular book is said to have been influential in the establishment of the national parks. During the Civil War, vigorously opposed to slavery but unable to fight for the Union due to his health, his organizational prowess resulted in his appointment as director of the United States Sanitary Commission, treating wounded soldiers and looking after their well-being.

Olmsted believed deeply that people can be influenced by their environment. He was captivated by the gardens and scenery of Europe, particularly a public park outside of Liverpool that was accessible to everyone. Later, when designing New York's Central Park, he wanted to create a space where people could escape and leave the stress of the city behind them. Parks were valuable places for people migrating from rural to metropolitan life. He regarded landscape design as an instrument of social change, a means to strengthen democracy and to establish a sense of community. "Each individual adding by his mere presence to the pleasure of all others, all helping to the greater happiness of each. You may thus often see vast numbers of persons brought closely together, poor and rich, young and old, Jew and Gentile."

The heart of Olmsted's vision was to let the natural beauty of a place come through and he believed that the design and added structures should be purposeful, enhancing the space and not be added simply for their own sakes. All the elements should collectively achieve a relaxing effect, an understanding evident in his preference for pastoral landscapes of meadows, small lakes, and groves of trees.

People of faith often lean toward the idea that the earth reflects a purposeful design, one that suggests that the beauty we see is not simply accidental but thought out with intentionality and attention to detail. The biblical authors were certain that God was a God of order and not chaos. For these writers, God measured the foundations of the earth, set the course for the waters to run, established boundaries to contain the seas, and decided upon the height of the mountains the way an architect today might draw a blueprint.

Science and religion do not necessarily need to be viewed as being in conflict on this matter. Who is to say that the Divine creative imagination and the process of gradual change are not related to the beauty we see in the world around us? After all, Olmsted believed that any quality design did not call attention to itself but rather allowed for a space to have its own genius.

Where do you see beauty in the world? What is your favorite park or landscape to visit for reducing your stress or for contemplation? How does your life contribute to the beauty of the world?

Central Park in New York City, considered one of Frederick Law Olmsted's greatest works

An example of purposeful design in Central Park

PICTURED ROCKS
NATIONAL LAKESHORE

MICHIGAN • 1966 • PATIENCE

The end of something is better than its beginning.
Patience is better than arrogance.
—Ecclesiastes 7:8 (CEB)

Of America's great landforms—the Rocky Mountains, the Appalachians, the coasts, the Mississippi and Missouri and Ohio and Columbia rivers and so many more—the Great Lakes don't get the attention they deserve. Maybe it's because the lakes are on the periphery of our geography. Or maybe it's because winter's grip on the lakes is tight and lengthy. They split the state of Michigan, creating an Upper Peninsula (UP) that is culturally and topographically different than its far-more-populated southern sibling. Perched atop the "UP" along the Lake Superior shore is Pictured Rocks National Lakeshore. Seeing the sights from the best vantage point takes patience—and a boat. Once you arrive, though, the splendor you see results from years and years of patient work by the basic forces that shape our planet.

Spread across a forty-two-mile-long stretch of Lake Superior shoreline, Painted Rocks displays the stark colors that are the result of millions of years of geological transition and centuries of groundwater seep. The result is a line of cliffs with crisscrossing colors carved into striking shapes by the relentless pounding of the largest Great Lake.

The beauty begins with soft, malleable sandstone. The oldest rock is sedimentary Jacobsville Sandstone, primarily rust-colored due to iron oxides but speckled with browns, whites, pinks, and white spheres and streaks created by water leeching out minerals. Above that is the softer gray-white Munising formation, then the Au Train formation, more resistant to erosion. By themselves, the trio of rocks would be

Kakayers dwarfed by towering cliffs

Miners Falls

beautiful as water and wind carve away at the exposed rock over the lake. But there's more happening beneath the surface.

As water soaks into the ground and the rock below, it dissolves minerals and slowly, patiently, carries them down the rock. When the water emerges from a cliff face, the minerals are deposited, flowing down as gravity pulls them. The different minerals are different colors, so the streaks are different colors, too. Iron leaves red and orange, copper green and blue, manganese black and brown, limonite white. The horizontal rock patterns, the vertical drips, and the shapes etched out of the limestone create an awe-inspiring artwork of geological splendor.

Because the cliffs are at the water's edge, the best vantage points of the cliffs float. Boat tours offer an easy way to see much of the park, and kayaking provides a more strenuous adventure. The shoreline has several landmarks, including Battleship Row, the Grand Portal tunnel through a cliff, Spray Falls and Sable Falls, and Miners Castle. One of the turrets from Miners Castle collapsed unexpectedly in 2008, a

Autumn

warning that approaching the rocks is a bad idea. Soft sandstone can give way, crashing tons of rocks into the lake, a spectacular sight evoking glaciers calving their ice.

Atop the cliffs are streams, lakes, and forests with a hundred miles of trails to explore. In the center of the park is Beaver Basin Wilderness, undeveloped and intended to recreate the quiet solitude of the northern woods. When autumn arrives, the colors can outdo the vibrancy of the cliffs. When the durable upper Au Train layer yields to the relentless flow of water, the resulting falls are worth the hike. As you watch water tumbling over Miners Falls or Mosquito

The cliffs of Battleship Row

Falls or Chapel Falls, consider how long it has taken nature to create that view, and know that on a microscopic level, it has changed ever so slightly during those few minutes you watched. At the end of the day, when it's time to relax back along the lakefront, beaches and sand dunes provide a place to play or sit as the sun slowly sets into the lake.

Pictured Rocks is the kind of park where you want to breathe it all in, hold your breath, then exhale slowly, pushing out the hustle and bustle of a see-it-all kind of day. Painstakingly slow water seeping through rocks at least half a billion years old created what we see today. All this by a lake that lies in an ancient rift between tectonic plates. It takes a lot of patience to create something this beautiful. Patience is a virtue overdue for a revival.

Grand Portal Point

When has being patient created a good result in your life? In what part of your life do you need to create or find more patience? When is patience not necessarily the best approach to a challenge?

The view from Mount Rose Trail overlook

GRAND PORTAGE
NATIONAL MONUMENT

MINNESOTA • 1958 • SEEDS

[Jesus] put before them another parable: "The kingdom of heaven is like a
mustard seed that someone took and sowed in his field; it is the smallest of all the
seeds, but when it has grown it is the greatest of shrubs and becomes a tree,
so that the birds of the air come and make nests in its branches."

MATTHEW 13:31–32 (NRSV)

The footpath is 8.5 miles, and when traveling from east to west, rises over 630 feet from the far western waters of Lake Superior to the Pigeon River. If you plan to hike the trail, expect a ten to twelve-hour round-trip excursion. Pack plenty of water, carry copious amounts of bug spray, and wear sturdy shoes to trek across the rocky terrain and wet soil.

The Grand Portage or "Great Carrying Place" was the water route link between *Gichigami*, the Ojibwa name for Lake Superior, and the northwestern territories of Canada. First Nation peoples, then the French, and later the British transported furs and other agricultural goods by canoe for trade across the northern tier of North America, encompassing the watersheds of Hudson Bay and the St. Lawrence River.

During the summer months in the late eighteenth century, there may have been as many as two thousand people gathered between the great lodge at Fort George on Lake Superior and at the river in Fort Charlotte. Grand Portage was one of four major trading posts for the British and the North West Company, with others being Fort Niagara, Fort Detroit, and Michilimackinac. Not just furs came across the path; as the population grew, so did demands for goods from Europe, tobacco from South America, even silk and cotton from China.

Grand Portage became a global merchandise exchange. Like the

Recreation of the "Three Sisters" garden: beans, corn, and squash

ancient people before them, the items for trade also included seeds. The historical "Three Sisters" garden at the national monument celebrates vegetable varieties of corn, beans, and squash whose origins are two hundred years old. Peas and parsnips came into the Native American diet from European traders, and squash, corn, and beans were likewise adopted by the voyagers as they traveled the trade route and took goods home.

The dietary changes reflected a greater cooperation that was necessary for survival. Ranger talks share how the Ojibwa taught trappers and traders when the whitefish were running, when and which crops would produce a harvest, where to find caribou, and how they mapped the best routes for travel westward. This history represents other seeds that have led to Grand Portage Monument being the only National Park Service unit to share the management of the land with Native Americans who actually donated the land to the Park Service. Under the Indian Self-Governance Act, the park is jointly overseen by NPS and the Grand Portage Band of the Lake Superior Chippewa Indian Nation. By this agreement, a joint mission of both historical preservation and cultural conservation are carried out on this land. Visitors see and experience the Grand Portage native culture as presented by the Chippewa Nation, which simultaneously seeks to maintain its spoken language and customs through the establishment of a charter school. It is a pathway to seed the future with the existential memories of the past.

Seeds also figure into another of the lesser-known missions of the National Park Service. Grand Portage is undergoing an ethnobotanical restoration, which includes restoring indigenous plants and also the human relationship and interaction with the plants. The southern boreal forest within the monument is being replenished with the planting of white pines and the use of wildland fires to manage and assist in the harvest of sweetgrass.

Each August, coinciding with the Perseid meteor shower, there is a rendezvous reenactment. A tradition across North America, the rendezvous was a time at which the trading companies hosted fur trappers who sold their pelts and resupplied for the next season. At the same time, the Grand Portage Indian Reservation hosts a powwow—a social gathering for the tribe to sing, dance, and honor their traditions. Grand Portage celebrates a relationship sown by acts of kindness by Native Americans to European trappers, two symbiotic parts of a thriving industry that, through trade, brought the world to the western edge of the frontier.

Ojibwa village recreation

Can you think of small actions that have blossomed into something much larger? From whose seeds have you harvested fruit? What seeds are you planting for future generations?

NATCHEZ TRACE
NATIONAL SCENIC TRAIL

MISSISSIPPI , ALABAMA, AND TENNESSEE • 1983 • PILGRIMAGE

Now that same day two of them were going to a village called Emmaus,
about seven miles from Jerusalem. They were talking with each other about
everything that had happened. As they talked and discussed these things with
each other, Jesus himself came up and walked along with them;
but they were kept from recognizing him.

—LUKE 24:13–16 (NIV)

Setting out on a trip, an adventure, to reach a distant destination where fortune awaited at the end of the road *if you could just get there*, a trek like the epic stories of the Bible—for many in the early 1800s United States, that destination was Natchez, Mississippi.

Perched on a bluff overlooking the vast Mississippi River, Natchez was already an old town, for centuries a Native American gathering place before French colonists recast it in their own image in 1716. It changed hands from France to Spain to Great Britain to the United States, but its role as a center of commerce and a worldly village, a place where Americans and Native Americans and Africans and emigrants crossed paths, made it one of the most important cities in the American Southwest.

Natchez's economy and wealth were tied to the rich farmland, which produced cotton and sugarcane on the backs of African American slave labor. Harvests went downstream, with the current, to New Orleans and on to the rest of the world. Fighting the current and heading north . . . well, that wasn't so easy. For decades, river traders would bring their crops to Natchez, sell them to the best bidder, and then walk home to the Ohio River valley. They followed the Natchez Trace, a trail more

Old Trace milepost 221.4

Frozen Fall Hollow waterfall

than four hundred miles long stretching to Nashville, Tennessee. In its day, it was like an interstate highway, the fastest way to travel on dry land.

Like all fabled roads, the Natchez Trace had its share of landmarks: prehistoric Native American mounds, waterfalls, scenic views, and the odd site of the "Sunken Trace" where the trail descended into soft ground, a groove worn by thousands of passing pedestrians. Like every highway, it offered services for travelers: ferries, taverns, inns, and stores. Like the National Road that crossed the Midwest, the Natchez Trace made traveling the fledgling country much easier.

When steam enabled commerce to travel upstream, Natchez continued to prosper. Wealthy landowners built mansions in and around the area, helping to create the image of the kind of Southern plantation that comes to mind when we read Faulkner or watch *Gone With The Wind*. We can see that splendor today in Melrose, mansion of the John T. McMurran family. But we also see the life of many free African Americans who lived in the area in the home of William Johnson, a freed slave who ended up owning several slaves of his own. A barber, Johnson taught his

Thousands of footsteps dug this groove in the Potkopinu section of the Natchez Trace.

trade to young freed slaves and kept a detailed diary for sixteen years. Both Johnson's home, where he and wife, Ann, lived with their eleven children, and the McMurran family mansion at Melrose are parts of the same park, a stark contrast considering what both families likely considered success.

As railroads supplanted steamboats at the turn of the twentieth century, Natchez faded in prominence, but as a site for seeing a cross section of Southern life before and after the Civil War, Natchez remains a draw. Today, we still travel to Natchez.

The Bible is full of stories of pilgrimages, travels with a sacred purpose: Moses up Mount Sinai, Israel's multiple returns to their home-land, young Jesus's family to Jerusalem, Jesus's entry into Jerusalem during the Jewish holy days, Paul's ministry across the Mediterranean, and so many more. The people in the Bible seemed constantly on the move! Millions of Christians visit the Holy Land or the Vatican each year. Clearly, there's something compelling about a pilgrimage.

Americans are people drawn to travel. Our vast highway system makes transcontinental travel easy; one could drive the 3,300 miles from Seattle to Miami in a week. Interstates make it easy to miss God's work off the beaten path. Often we travel fast, too focused on reaching the destination to take a moment to look around and take in the beauty around us, natural and human alike.

Mount Locust Historic House, built around 1780

If you have gone on a pilgrimage, where did you go? How did that pilgrimage change you? If you would like to go on a pilgrimage, where would you go and why?

Boy Carver statue
by Robert Amendola

GEORGE WASHINGTON CARVER
NATIONAL MONUMENT

MISSOURI • 1943 • CURIOSITY

People were bringing little children to Jesus for him to place his hands on them,
but the disciples rebuked them. When Jesus saw this, he was indignant.
He said to them, "Let the little children come to me, and do not hinder them,
for the kingdom of God belongs to such as these. Truly I tell you, anyone who
will not receive the kingdom of God like a little child will never enter it."
And he took the children in his arms, placed his hands on them and blessed them.
—MARK 10:13-16 (NIV)

History recalls George Washington Carver as "the peanut man," a brilliant botanist who gave humanity more than a hundred ways to use the ubiquitous legume. But Carver the scientist was also an artist and a man whose faith shaped his outlook on his life's work.

Born a slave in southwest Missouri during the Civil War, George, his mother, and brother were kidnapped when he was just a week old. He and his brother were rescued, but not his mother. His owners, Moses and Susan Carver, raised George themselves, and Susan taught him until he was old enough to attend a school for African American children.

Carver was a frail child, unfit for the physically challenging work of the farm that produced oats, corn, hay, fruit, livestock, and other crops. Instead, when finished with household chores, Carver roamed their farm—a land that ignited his curiosity. Fetching spring water, Carver dawdled, as all kids do, playing in the stream and examining the animals and plants around him. In those woods, Carver planted his first garden, hidden in the brush, a place to tend flowers, experiment with plants, and dig into the rich soil. He collected the prettiest pebbles he found in the spring. It's easy to imagine George's pockets

George Washington Carver, circa 1910

full of stones, his hands cradling a croaking frog or a sprig of delicate wildflowers.

That farm is also where Carver found his faith. He recalled a day when he was ten years old: "God just came into my heart one afternoon while I was alone in the loft of our big barn while I was shelling corn." A neighbor boy told him about prayer, and soon Carver found himself inspired. "I do not recall what I said. I only recall that I felt so good that I prayed several times before I quit."

George Washington Carver National Monument recreates that boyhood playground. The farm looks different now, its main home relocated and the small slave quarters where George was born destroyed by a tornado. The spring has been dammed into a small lake and the

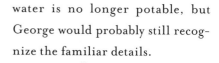

Carver explored this creek as a child.

water is no longer potable, but George would probably still recognize the familiar details.

Carver later moved to Kansas, then to college in Iowa, before joining the faculty at Tuskegee Institute, the preeminent Alabama college for African Americans in the era of segregation. There he was an educator, scientist, and public servant, sharing lessons about agriculture with a developing nation. His worked focused on cotton, potatoes, sweet potatoes, and of course peanuts, as well as modernizing agricultural practices, but he was also a painter who learned that Alabama clay made rich, durable paints—and patented a process for creating more than five hundred shades. His love for painting was inspired by those creek-bed pebbles.

Moses Carver house

"Most of the things I do are just cookery," said the scientist who routinely took a devotional walk at four o'clock each afternoon. "These are not my products. God put them here and I found them."

That faith imbued Carver with a compassionate spirit. "How far you go in life depends on your being tender with the young, compassionate with the aged, sympathetic with the striving, and tolerant of the weak and the strong. Because someday in life you will have been all of these."

Carver's work transcended racial lines, and his view of his faith transcended the lines of human understanding. "Someday I will have to leave this world. And when that day comes I want to feel that I have an excuse for having lived in it. I want to feel that my life has been of some service to my fellow man."

It's fitting that the first National Park Service unit honoring an African American preserved the playground of a very curious boy.

What are the curious moments that have shaped your life? What would you like to know more about now? How do you help the curious children in your life?

A turtle in Williams Pond

LITTLE BIGHORN BATTLEFIELD
NATIONAL MONUMENT

MONTANA • 1879 • REASON

There is a way that appears to be right,

but in the end it leads to death.

—PROVERBS 14:12 (NIV)

A century and a half later, we're still unsure of the precise events of the afternoon of June 25, 1876, at Little Bighorn, a battlefield in the southeastern Montana prairies. History records that a celebrated military leader made several bad decisions and lost a battle to Native Americans whose way of life was under attack.

Today, we can walk through Little Bighorn Battlefield National Monument, trying to understand from both the Native American and the US military points of view what happened and why, imagining the combat and the terror that occurred there that summer day. But we will never know for sure what actually occurred.

Here's what we do know: since before the Civil War, the United States had attempted to subdue Native American tribes of the northern Plains by treaties and by force. The winter thaw of 1876 saw George Armstrong Custer and his subordinates pursuing Sioux and Cheyenne warriors who had left their reservations and moved west into the Crow reservation in the Yellowstone River valley. They were engaged in the Sun Dance, a ritual gathering involving personal sacrifice for the greater good. The government's hope was to get the tribe to return to their allotments.

As June wound down, Custer's forces were closing in on an encampment on the Little Bighorn River. Custer believed the right engagement would force the Native Americans to return to the reservations.

Grave markers at Little Bighorn Battlefield

George Armstrong Custer

History records that Custer made several key misjudgments. He underestimated how many Sioux and Cheyenne, warriors and noncombatants, were in the valley. He also assumed he would be able to capture women, children, and the elderly, and use their release as a bargaining chip with tribal leaders. Custer was also extremely confident in his soldiers' abilities to handle anything the Native Americans could throw at them. He assumed that two subordinates, Major Marcus Reno and Captain Frederick Benteen, would be willing and able to provide effective support.

Custer formulated his plan: Reno would drive up the river, Custer would stay on the high ground. Approaching from the south, Benteen would arrive in time to provide support. Following his commander's plan, Reno attacked the camp but retreated as the Sioux and Cheyenne reacted. Withdrawing to higher ground, Reno and Benteen dug defensive positions.

Three miles north, Custer was in trouble, and he signaled that he needed assistance. That assistance never came, and Custer's men paid with their lives. Trapped on a hilltop, overwhelmed and vulnerable, not a single American soldier survived what happened next. Known now as Custer's Last Stand, the Seventh Cavalry died in a brief, gruesome battle.

Reno and Benteen's units escaped, and the Sioux and

Cheyenne River Sioux Riders

118

Cheyenne camp quickly dispersed. A few days later, once the area had cleared out, soldiers returned to the battlefield to discover the carnage. In all, 268 American soldiers died at Little Bighorn. Native American casualties were uncountable because most of the bodies had already been removed. The American dead were buried, and the morbid news was shared with a country celebrating its centennial.

In the years that followed, many professional scholars and amateur historians tried to retrace Custer's steps. Several contradictory stories emerged, both from the Native Americans present that day and from the military inquiries that followed. Sleuths continue theorizing today, but no matter: the result is as obvious as the tombstones marking where combatants from both sides fell.

Custer didn't correctly assess the odds against him. Why had he been so eager to engage a force he badly misread? Why had he been so aggressive? Why did he overestimate his troops' ability? Had Custer continued to make poor choices in a vain attempt to regain the upper hand, or had soldiers panicked and the command structure collapsed? Why hadn't Reno and Benteen responded to the calls for help? The what-ifs are endless.

In the biblical creation story, God gives humans reason, the ability to think logically about an action and its consequences. Much of the time, we make reasonable choices. Reason takes us far down the path presented by each option. But when we panic, when we follow our more primal instincts, we lose our ability to reason. We surrender that first cognitive gift God gave us.

When has thinking through the possibilities made a difference in your life? When has panicking cost you? What helps you stay calm and reasonable when you feel the need to panic?

Stormy skies over the battlefield

HOMESTEAD NATIONAL MONUMENT OF AMERICA

NEBRASKA • 1936 • WORTHINESS

*To this end we always pray for you, asking that our God will make you worthy of
his call and will fulfill by his power every good resolve and work of faith.*
—2 THESSALONIANS 1:11 (NRSV)

Free land! This was the promise of the Homestead Act, signed
into law by Abraham Lincoln in 1862. One hundred sixty acres
awaited anyone who was over twenty-one or the head of a household
and willing to move to the untamed and expanding American West.
The law intended to accomplish two things: to settle the West, and to
give economic opportunity to anyone willing to work hard, regardless
of race, national origin, or gender.

The Homestead Act reflects Lincoln's approach to the function
of the federal government. In a speech on July 4, 1861, he said that
government's purpose is "to elevate the condition of men, to lift arti-
ficial burdens from all shoulders and to give everyone an unfettered
start and a fair chance in the race of life." When viewed in the context of
immigration, of those formerly enslaved, or of women seeking self-determination, it is hard to underestimate the Homestead Act's impact.

Three hundred thousand immigrants benefited from the Bureau of
Land Management's largesse. Coming from Europe, they sought better
opportunity and the promise that their hard work would reward *them*
rather than noblemen or monarchies. Women also filed for land claims,
though since the head of household provision was limited to men, a
woman had to be single or forego marriage for the duration of the
five-year residency requirement to be eligible for land. A special clause
allowed widows of Union soldiers to deduct the time their husbands
had served in the Civil War from the five-year residency requirement.

Palmer-Epard cabin, built in 1867,
was moved to Homestead in 1950.

To survive on the prairie, a windmill was a necessity for water. Dempster windmills were considerecd the best and most innovative.

Stories of female homesteaders like Mattie Oblinger and the Chrisman sisters have been preserved, setting a high standard for courage and fortitude.

Freed slaves sought to risk the adversity and hardship of homesteading, believing that if they survived life in bondage, they surely could endure the frontier. From the end of the Civil War to the end of Reconstruction, there was a large westward exodus from the Southern states. From these "exodusters" communities like Blackdom, New Mexico; Dearfield, Colorado; DeWitty, Nebraska; and Nicodemus, Kansas, rose and fell, demonstrating the mix of success and failure of these ventures. Bad weather, crop-devouring insects, unscrupulous businessmen, and the land itself seemed to seem to work against them.

All 1.6 million of the sodbusters who sought to make a claim on the 270 million acres of land eventually given out through the Homestead Act found that the seemingly simple requirements of sowing and living on the land for five years were not so easy after all. From 1862, when Daniel Freeman became the first person to pay his fee and file a claim, to the year 1900, only 52 percent of claim filers successfully "proved up," meeting and verifying the

A plough, the "sodbusting" tool of the homesteader on the prairie

minimum requirements. Grant applications slowed through the early twentieth century, and the Homestead Act was brought to a close in May of 1976, though a ten-year extension was given to those willing to go to Alaska. Ken Deardorff did just that, and he is recognized as the last homesteader, receiving his land patent in 1988.

For all the original Homestead Act accomplished in opening the West and creating opportunity, it also nearly eradicated Native Americans, pushing them from their ancestral grounds onto reservations with little or no compensation. Poor farming techniques and a failure to understand the Great Plains ecosystem contributed to the Dust Bowl conditions of the 1930s. Any reflection on the Homestead Act should ponder how policies driven solely by economic considerations can have unintended, tragic, and far-reaching consequences.

For the men and women who accepted the task to cultivate and settle the land, it was more than the land that was "proved up." It took incredible resolve and discipline to take up the government's challenge. Whether it was met with success or failure, these were people to be admired. For those awarded a land patent, they had run the gauntlet and proven themselves worthy of the 160 acres. It is like undertaking the goal to grow in discipleship, enduring the difficulty of doubt and the trial of personal failings to gain strength in grace and to stand in confidence that our striving to do good makes us worthy to be counted among the faithful.

The architecture of the Heritage Center is reminiscent of a prairie schooner.

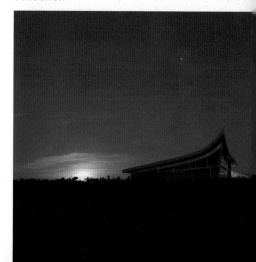

When have you endured a struggle that had a positive outcome? In what ways do you work on your faith with a similar resolve as the homesteaders "proving up"? How does prayer help your determination?

Black Canyon at Lake Mead

LAKE MEAD
NATIONAL RECREATION AREA

NEVADA • 1964 • RECREATION

*[Jesus] said to them, "Come away to a deserted place all by yourselves and rest
a while." For many were coming and going, and they had no leisure even to eat.*
—MARK 6:31 (NRSV)

The Lake Mead National Recreation Area covers over 200,000
acres of land and is heralded as both the largest and the most
diverse of all of our National Recreation Areas. Lake Mead and Lake
Mojave are oases of life-giving water, surrounded by three of the four
desert ecosystems in the United States: the Great Basin, the Mojave,
and the Sonoran deserts. Created by damming the Colorado River
with the Davis and Hoover Dams, sixty-seven miles apart, the lakes
together cover 186,000 acres, most of the area's total landmass. The
waters provide opportunities for boating, water sports, fishing, and
swimming. For the growing cities of the American Southwest, the lakes
are the source of power generation, drinking water, irrigation, and
flood control and impact the Southwest from Las Vegas to Tucson and
Los Angeles to Mexico. Serving millions of people takes its toll on the
water supply; coupled with an ongoing drought, the lake hasn't been
filled to capacity for decades.

But there is more than the water that draws people here. Wilderness
areas for hiking, off-roading, camping, and general exploring dot the
landscape around the water's edge. Encounters with numerous species
of birds, plants, and animals await the curious traveler. Despite all the
water, this is the desert, and sojourners venturing out on the trails are
encouraged to take plenty of water as summer days easily exceed 100
degrees Fahrenheit.

Tourists come for the boating and hiking but also to see the cause of

Hiking Owl Canyon

the Colorado's transformation from a waterway that sliced out the Grand Canyon a few dozen miles east into the stream that created North America's largest reservoir. Known originally as Boulder Dam, it was renamed for President Hoover in 1947. Spanning the Black Canyon that separates Arizona from Nevada, the Hoover Dam represents one of the greatest feats of engineering of its day. The logistics alone of getting supplies from nearby Las Vegas to the construction site were staggering, requiring several railroad lines whose enormous tunnels through volcanic rock are now part of a national hiking trail that provides breathtaking views of Lake Mead and its surrounding shoreline. The power generated by the dam has not only paid for the entire project, it also underwrites the millions of dollars needed annually to maintain the 726-foot-tall structure and adjacent buildings.

Lake Mead National Recreation Area is more than a playground for the 7.5 million visitors each year who seek fun and sport or a tour of the dam. For scientists, it is a living laboratory. The study of everything from migratory birds to native species of fish, forced to adapt from life in a free-flowing seasonally warm river to a deep, cool lake is ongoing and year-round.

The calm water and sandy beach at Cottonwood Cove

The idea of rest and renewal is as ancient as the earth. An entire day of creation, according to Genesis 2:1–3, is dedicated to the idea of a day off. Imagine a Divinely sanctioned day not to be worried about schedules, the demands of an employer, the necessities of hunting and gathering, doing mundane chores, or fulfilling obligations to others. A day dedicated to goofing off and being with your family *because God said* so! Being faithful actually *requires* you to cease your regular activities so that you can remember that the world doesn't exist just because of your frenetic activity. The Sabbath story is the reminder that *you are not* God and there is enough of everything that earth produces as a providential gift for your sustenance.

Lake Mead's most famous landmark: Hoover Dam

When Jesus invites his close followers to "get away," he is reminding them that the labor will wait and that rest is necessary. A tired and worn body cannot deploy its best gifts or function at its highest capacity. There is a diminishing return to a soul spent in service to others. There really might be such a thing as compassion fatigue, and Jesus offers its antidote in time for rest and relaxation. This was his own practice, and one aspect of discipleship is to do as the teacher does.

Do you resist rest? If so, why? Have you ever been "spent past your capacity"? Can you remember a time when rest *now* made you more effective at work *later*?

Exploring one of the giant railway tunnels created to bring construction supplies to the site

SAINT-GAUDENS NATIONAL HISTORIC PARK

NEW HAMPSHIRE • 1966 • CREATIVITY

The LORD spoke to Moses: Look, I have chosen Bezalel, Uri's son and Hur's grandson from the tribe of Judah. I have filled him with the divine spirit, with skill, ability, and knowledge for every kind of work. He will be able to create designs; do metalwork in gold, silver, and copper; cut stones for setting; carve wood; and do every kind of work.

—EXODUS 31:1–5 (CEB)

We are accustomed to seeing art within the setting where it is on display: in a museum, in a home, in a public space, and so on. Rarely do we get the opportunity to see where the art itself was created—first the vision, then an experiment, and at last the final product. Saint-Gaudens National Historical Park is one of those places where we can see the artist's home and inspiration on display for all, just like the finished work.

At the turn of the twentieth century, Augustus Saint-Gaudens was perhaps the country's most beloved sculptor. Raised in New York City and educated in Europe, Saint-Gaudens had both the bold vision and the attention to detail to create some of the country's most iconic sculptures, from monuments adorning city parks to the coins carried in our pockets.

You've probably seen Saint-Gaudens' work without realizing it. He broke onto the artistic scene with his 1881 sculpture of Civil War Admiral David Farragut in New York City. In the following years he created statues of two Union generals: William T. Sherman, placed near Central Park, and John A. Logan in Chicago. His sculpture of Abraham Lincoln, *Standing Lincoln*, located in Lincoln Park in Chicago, is considered one of the finest portrait sculptures ever made, worthy

New Gallery's atrium
and pool

Augustus Saint-Gaudens, 1905

of replicas being placed at Lincoln's tomb, in London's Parliament Square, and in Parque Lincoln in Mexico City.

Perhaps his best-known work is Boston's *Robert Gould Shaw Memorial*. Commemorating the Massachusetts 54th Regiment, among the first battalion of African American soldiers, the memorial is striking in its accuracy, a testament to Saint-Gaudens's focus. The sculptor worked meticulously to represent the troops accurately; he hired forty African American models and captured their physical characteristics, a move atypical of the artistic portrayals of the time and reflecting a new perception of the country. No wonder the sculpture took nearly fourteen years to complete—and it was worth every second.

Saint-Gaudens summered at his home in Cornish beginning in 1885 and moved there permanently in 1900. Many other creators joined him; for two decades, the Cornish Art Colony buzzed with painters, writers, actors, musicians, and dancers. The sculptor named his house Aspet, after his French father's birthplace, and it became an artistic palace that serves as the heart of today's park.

Replica of Saint-Gaudens's famous *Shaw Memorial*

With its manicured gardens, hedges, and greens, the estate befits an artist who must have imagined three-dimensional shapes and forms all around him. In the studio where he worked in his later years, we can imagine the noise of sculpting, the quiet concentration of the artist contemplating his next move in the medium, and the intense heat and the metallic scent of melted bronze. More than a hundred pieces of artwork are displayed at the park, continuing the artistic inspiration Saint-Gaudens and others found there.

It's hard to put a price on that kind of inspiration, but a representative opening bid might have been twenty dollars. In 1904 President Theodore Roosevelt selected Saint-Gaudens to create new designs for American coinage. The twenty-dollar gold coin, dubbed the "double eagle," was one of the most elegant coins ever produced but so difficult to create that only a handful were ever minted. Today a single coin in excellent condition can fetch millions of dollars.

Artists are often depicted as self-centered, difficult to work with, best left alone with their creativity. Not Saint-Gaudens. An acclaimed teacher, he mentored young artists and had many apprentices in his work. His protégés included many of the most acclaimed sculptors of the early twentieth century.

You can be the newest Saint-Gaudens apprentice, learning the first steps of sculpting, mold making, and casting. Sculptors-in-residence share their craft and their stories with visitors. Walking the grounds and seeing life as an artist may give you a new perspective on an ordinary lump of clay or a rock that captures your imagination. Creativity is, as Bezalel in Scripture and the countless creators who followed Saint-Gaudens would assert, a blessing from God, not just to one person but to all those who experience the art.

Pan Pool with Mount Ascutney in the background

How do you express your creativity? Who in your life is your creative muse? Are you somebody else's muse?

Restored heavy machine shop

THOMAS EDISON
NATIONAL HISTORICAL PARK

NEW JERSEY • 1962 • TRANSFORMATION

*Do not be conformed to this world, but be transformed by the renewing of
your minds, that you may discern what is the will of God—
what is good and acceptable and perfect.*
—ROMANS 12:2 (NRSV)

Thomas Alva Edison is perhaps America's best known and most prolific inventor, acquiring over one thousand patents in his name. Born in 1847 into humble circumstances in Milan, Ohio, he is also one of the country's best entrepreneurial rags to riches stories, moving from being a twelve-year-old "news butcher" selling food and newspapers on trains and a "tramp telegrapher" for the railroads in his teens to becoming one of the original partners in General Electric.

Edison was also a hero of sorts as he saved the life of three-year-old Jimmy MacKenzie, who would have been struck by a runaway train had Thomas not intervened. Jimmy's father, a station agent, was so grateful that he taught the young Edison how to be a telegrapher. Edison used his time on the rails experimenting with chemicals in a boxcar until one of his experiments exploded! Edison and his laboratory were summarily thrown from the train by its conductor as it rolled across central Michigan.

Called a genius by his peers and granted such ascriptions as "The Wizard of Menlo Park" by the society pages, the ever-humble Edison asserted that "Genius is 1 percent inspiration and 99 percent perspiration." He was afraid of neither hard work nor failure. To Edison, experimentation was simply a way to learn.

Anecdotally Edison is credited with numerous inventions, including the lightbulb, motion pictures, and commercial electrical power

Thomas Alva Edison

generation. Yet Edison was not in fact the originator of many of these things—including the lightbulb. What he did do was significantly improve upon existing designs. The one exception is his patent on the phonograph, the first machine ever to record sound. Given that Edison was deaf in one ear and couldn't hear well out of the other, there is a touch of irony that we have him to thank for the record player.

He is lesser known for his contributions to alkaline batteries, Portland cement, X-rays, and a host of military innovations including early forms of sonar and radar, anti-roll platforms for ships to stabilize gun mounts, as well as anti-rust coatings for submarines.

A visit to the park at West Orange means a visit to Glenmont, Edison's home and the laboratory where he and hundreds of "muckers" worked in the art and craft of experimentation. Under the hum of electric motors turning overhead steel shafts that pulled leather belts driving machines on the factory floor below, the lab became the forerunner of modern industrial research and development. Standing on the polished hardwood of the Edison laboratory, you are at the birthplace of the home appliance revolution that changed American home and office life in the

Edicraft toaster, an early American modern kitchen appliance

twentieth century. You also occupy space where people with last names like Ford, Tesla, Latimer, Hammer, and Johnson partnered with Edison early in their careers.

Edison's work and methodology has had a lasting impact reaching into our century. Imagine life without the lightbulb, recorded music, or motion pictures. His list of patents impacts everything from the fluoroscope used at your doctor's office to the Pyrex used in your kitchen! The story *behind* the story of Edison is one of hungering to know more in order to *be* more. He was driven by a desire to succeed in industry through innovation. For him, there was always more that could be achieved with determination and new information learned through experimentation.

The music room is where recordings were made and the reproductions enjoyed.

There is something to be said with not being satisfied with what is known, choosing to be something better, greater, and more than what one is in the current moment. The Apostle Paul encourages members of the church at Rome to live their faith in this same spirit. Don't just settle for where you are now in your faith; be eager to be *more*. Be transformed. Take what is, and, in the company of others, work with them to create the best that can possibly be. Challenge yourself and others to make a difference. What could be a better description of a community of people engaged together in the work of discipleship?

Glenmont, the Edison home

Where and how do you practice collaboration and with whom? What have you achieved by working with others? How is the collective wisdom of others improving you and your ability to make a difference?

BANDELIER
NATIONAL MONUMENT

NEW MEXICO • 1916 • SHELTER

While they were there, the time came for [Mary] to deliver her child.
And she gave birth to her firstborn son and wrapped him in bands of cloth,
and laid him in a manger, because there was no place for them in the inn.

LUKE 2:6–7 (NRSV)

Finding Bandelier National Monument would be tough if you didn't know where it was. Tucked into walls of a canyon etched by a Rio Grande tributary, Bandelier is a reminder of what a neighborhood looked like in the American Southwest a thousand years ago. Many Native American settlements remain in the area, several still active, and the National Park Service manages several historic sites. Bandelier, though, gives us a close-up glimpse of that life.

Bandelier exists first because of volcanic eruptions more than a million years ago that spewed ash over a huge swath of land. That ash cooled into tuff, a soft and light rock that is easily eroded by water and wind and easily excavated and used for construction. Harder basalt made for strong tools, and the ponderosa pines provided strong structural supports. The Ancestral Pueblo combined these resources to create their homes, carving rooms called *cavates* into the cliff face of Cañon de los Frijoles and crafting bricks for walls.

For centuries, the community was tucked away in the canyon, but it was not isolated. Archaeologists have uncovered evidence of a trade network stretching into Mexico. But after four hundred years, the surrounding land could no longer support Bandelier's population, and a drought settled in. Residents dispersed to the southeast along the Rio Grande, where their descendants dwell to this day.

Centuries later, during the Great Depression, Bandelier benefited

Inside a cavate

Climb inside Cave Kiva on recreated ladders.

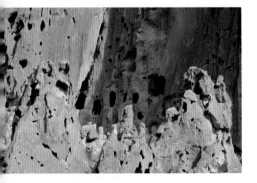

The soft rock of the canyon is riddled with holes, perfect for excavation.

greatly from the Civilian Conservation Corps, a work program that employed thousands of young men, in so doing protecting them from homelessness and training them for skilled labor. The park has two complementary architectural styles in one park: one evoking a civilization that has faded but not vanished, another the "Parkitecture" we identify with the shared sacred spaces of the National Park System.

Today at Bandelier, we walk the same paths that the pueblo's inhabitants used for more than 11,000 years. We climb into the same rooms where they celebrated, mourned, and lived for centuries, seeing the soot from their fires that cemented the rock ceilings. In some places we see their paintings and petroglyphs on the walls. We take in the same breathtaking views of the canyon from their doorways and windows. We imagine smelling the food cooking over flame and hearing their laughter as they recount the events of the day or their concern that there isn't enough food for everybody. There are signs that the community cared for the sick in the pueblos. Life was hard in these places; the average life expectancy was only thirty-five years.

New Mexican weather has its extremes — scorching in the summer, frigid in the winter, gulley-washers a threat to everything downstream. When we climb the ladders to get to Alcove House, 140 feet above the canyon floor, we can break a sweat or feel the cold wind on exposed skin, but we are escaping the danger of a flooding stream or an approaching enemy. When we duck our head and crawl inside a cavate, we feel the rock's coolness in the summer or the warmth of shelter from the winter wind. We can wait out a storm, tidy and dry, and rest. We imagine the families that lived in this place generations ago, appreciating being able to escape the elements.

Aspen along the Cerro Grande Route

Finding shelter is a common element in many biblical stories, but few stories in Christianity hold such emotional poignancy or such sensory power as the story of the birth of Jesus, the child of a couple on an unfortunately timed trek forced by a ruler assessing his power and wealth in the coming years. Joseph and Mary could find no place for them at the inn and took what they could get: a stable for animals. We feel their desperation and fear as Mary faced childbirth, a dangerous, sometimes fatal experience. We feel their relief as they settled into this shelter after Mary delivered her first child in this unfamiliar place, a gift—a blessing—from a stranger in a time of need.

Coyote at sunrise

When have you needed to find shelter during an emergency? When have you had the blessing of receiving shelter or support from an unexpected source? What qualities make your home more than a shelter?

The Great Hall on Ellis Island

STATUE OF LIBERTY NATIONAL MONUMENT

NEW YORK • 1933 • ALIEN

The alien who resides with you shall be to you as the citizen among you;
you shall love the alien as yourself, for you were aliens in the land of Egypt:
I am the LORD your God.

—LEVITICUS 19:34 (NRSV)

If America has a front door, it must be New York harbor. Following the Immigration Act of 1882, it became the largest legal entry point into the United States. Prior to that, America had no restrictions on persons coming to find their freedom or fortune. The Immigration Act itself placed a "head tax" on persons seeking entry and required that they not be "a convict, lunatic, idiot, or person likely to become a public charge." From 1892 to 1954, over twelve million immigrants passed through Ellis Island as they arrived in the United States.

Since 1886, "Liberty Enlightening the World" has stood as a silent sentinel welcoming to New York all who sought to make America their home. A gift from France celebrating both a long friendship between the countries and the abolition of slavery at the end of America's Civil War, the "lady with the lamp"— better known as the Statue of Liberty— has become a *global* symbol of freedom and democracy.

Most people recognize her by her torch and crown, others by the book, cradled tightly with her left arm, inscribed with the date of the United States' Declaration of Independence. For many, distinguishing this from all other landmarks is Emma Lazarus's poem fixed to the pedestal with words in bronze that welcome the world's "tired, poor, and huddled masses yearning to breathe free."

It is a considerably smaller number of people, however, who recognize what Édouard de Laboulaye, French political thinker and

New arrivals at Ellis island

abolitionist who first envisioned her, likely had in mind with her design. The copper colossus's special feature, mostly hidden beneath her flowing robe, is a *broken* chain. Lady Liberty does not stand still, but rather walks in full stride because the shackles fastened to her ankles can no longer hold her in one place. Laboulaye's Liberty marches forth with the light of freedom into a waiting world that gives the right of self-determination for *every* human person.

Her creation was intended to be a constant beacon to freedom and a light against the dark enslavement of others, whether through ownership or political tyranny. In this regard, some say Liberty has failed. While the official yoke of slavery was broken with the Union's victory in the Civil War, the full weight of that promise has yet to be realized by persons of African descent some 150 years later.

The openly Jim Crow South and the more covert but equaling crippling red-lined districts of the North kept the full experience of liberty from these Americans through the middle of the twentieth century.

Immigrants made their petition to come into America and her promise in the hearing room.

Now, in the early twenty-first century, we have come to realize that systemic oppression of minority groups is built into the very structures we have created to govern and administer our lives as a nation. In recent years, there has been increased movement toward building walls rather than creating doors for people to become a part of a great experiment that the Statue of Liberty represents—especially among the disadvantaged and the nonwhite global population. This is not new; we have placed such barriers before on groups seen as less than desirable, forgetting that every one of us who isn't Native American has come from some-place else.

To our own detriment we overlook that some of the greatest scientists, scholars, philosophers, artists, athletes, and inventors came to this country as immigrants

Lady Liberty at nightfall

with little more than the clothes on their backs. They enriched our lives by deepening the color palette from which we paint the story of our nation, adding to, rather than subtracting from, the resources we use to create our future.

At times, the lady in New York harbor represents more of a roman-tic ideal than an ever-present and deeply lived value. Yet she calls us still to be more than we are and to reach for what we, in our best moments, most want—to welcome others as we ourselves have been welcomed, to work for the freedom of others as hard as we work to preserve our own.

The feet of Liberty, chains broken, walking into freedom

When have you experienced being a stranger? What does it mean to be welcomed? How do you balance your citizenship in a nation and your citizenship in the Realm of God?

A bronze statue reenactment of the first flight adorns the monument grounds.

WRIGHT BROTHERS
NATIONAL MEMORIAL

NORTH CAROLINA • 1933 • INSPIRATION

But those who wait for the LORD shall renew their strength,
they shall mount up with wings like eagles,
they shall run and not be weary, they shall walk and not faint.

—ISAIAH 40:31 (NRSV)

Since the first humans looked to the sky and jealously witnessed birds winging overhead, we have wanted to fly. You've watched children flap their arms, imitating the birds as they run after them. You may remember holding out your own arms while coasting on your bicycle, pretending to soar.

No one knows when the first of our ancestors attempted to take to the firmament or how many lost their lives trying. Cave drawings dating back 4,500 years before the Common Era depict people with wings. More than three thousand years later, Greek mythology tells the story of Daedalus and Icarus taking to the sky with wings of wax, sticks, twine, and feathers, only for Icarus to fly too close to the heat of the sun and fall to his death. The Chinese are believed to have invented the kite as early as one thousand years before the birth of Christ. Ballooning was developed in France toward the end of the eighteenth century. But powered, heavier-than-air flight that could take a person some distance remained elusive.

As the twentieth century dawned, the ability to fly had not yet been realized, but the dream to do so and the inspiration to make it so were aided by rapidly advancing science and technology. Enter Orville and Wilbur Wright, sons of a leader in the United Brethren church, who lived in Dayton, Ohio. They were self-taught engineers and mechanics whose imaginations were sparked toward flying at an early age by a

Reproductions of the buildings that served as workshop, storage space, and home from 1900–1904

simple French-made toy that resembled a modern-day propeller. When spun at high speed, the toys climbed toward the heavens then fell back to earth. By day the Wright Brothers built and repaired bicycles, but their dream was to take to the sky, and they remained restless until they answered that call in 1899.

For the next four years, they observed the natural world, intensely studying birds in flight. They scoured the collective and recorded research of the day, including data from the Smithsonian Institution in Washington. They experimented with gliders, both with and without pilots. They chose the North Carolina shore for their test trials as it had three qualities they wanted: consistent wind for lift, privacy, and sand-covered hills providing elevation, few obstacles, and relatively soft landings. Each year, when winter drove them off the dunes and back to Ohio, they continued their research with a wind tunnel they constructed themselves.

Atop Kill Devil Hill sits a monument to the Wright brothers and powered human flight.

Every success inspired them to press on, and every failure challenged them to create a solution. Finally, on December 17, 1903, all their work culminated in the first recorded controlled powered flight of a heavier-than-air machine. Humanity had "slipped the surly bonds of earth" when Orville kept the plane aloft for twelve seconds and traveled 120 feet—a distance that would fit *inside* most modern commercial aircraft. The altitude and speed were not much to write home about by today's standards—but the fact that they had flown was global news!

They flew three more times that day, with the next flights' distance and duration increasing until a crash ended the day's experiments and winter closed their workshop for the season. Working back in Ohio, by 1905 they had achieved sustained,

A look at Orville's perspective as pilot

controlled flight for over thirty-eight minutes, and the ability to return to their point of origin. Shy of Edison perfecting the light bulb, it is hard to think about any invention that has had a greater impact in our everyday lives than what happened outside of Kitty Hawk in 1903. The modern era of flight had begun. In just six decades, humans would not only fly around the world, but set foot on the moon. The Wrights, once inspired by others, became an inspiration for others.

Flight is a metaphor for freedom. A desert-wandering people who heard Isaiah's words no doubt imagined what it would be like to get sandal-clad feet out of the burning sand. To soar like an eagle, to be the predator and not the prey. To enjoy speed, agility, beauty, perspective. To glide on the wind instead of bracing against it. Dreams like this have inspired us to achieve great things. What might be next?

If you could accomplish some great thing, what would it be and how would it change the world? In what ways are you an inspiration for others? What inspires you and why?

The Wright Flyer at liftoff (cast in bronze)

KNIFE RIVER INDIAN VILLAGES
NATIONAL HISTORIC SITE

NORTH DAKOTA • 1974 • HOSPITALITY

Do not forget to show hospitality to strangers, for by so doing some people have
shown hospitality to angels without knowing it.
—HEBREWS 13:2 (NIV)

Before airplanes arching across the azure skies could traverse the country in a few hours, before a grid of highways enabled us to cross the country in a few days, rivers were the quickest way to move to a new place. Native American settlements along the rivers were the first rest areas, places for travelers to find shelter, food, and human contact.

For hundreds of years, the Hidatsa lived at the confluence of the 2,300-mile-long Missouri River and its tributary, the Knife River, near the center of what we now call North Dakota. While many nomadic Native American tribes lived in *tipis*, the Hidatsa and their neighbors were farmers and traders, with no need to relocate regularly. They built permanent homes in settlements that exceeded a thousand residents. Today, the sites of three neighboring villages—Awatixa Xi'e, Awatixa, and Hidatsa Village—are preserved at Knife River Indian Villages National Historic Site.

The original homes no longer exist, but a reconstruction helps visitors imagine what used to occupy the circular indentations in the ground where countless footsteps compacted the soil. Construction of the domes was overseen by a woman who knew the required engineering and the sacred vision for building what was both a home and a holy place. The domed homes were ten to fifteen feet tall and thirty to sixty feet in diameter, covered in grass held in place by a ring of timber. A square doorway led to a small corral that could hold a few horses. Around the circle's perimeter were beds for about twenty people, a sweat lodge, and

A reconstructed Hidatsa earthlodge

Recreating a family's life inside an earthlodge

a shrine where only the men who owned holy relics could intrude. Food was cached along the wall and in the floor. In the center of the lodge was a fireplace surrounded by reed mats. A place of honor, the *atuka*, was reserved for the oldest man in the house but also for special visitors. Over the fireplace reached four pillars in which Hidatsa believed the spirit of the house lived; offerings of hide or cloth were often wrapped around the pillars.

For traders, location has always been key, and the Hidatsa had an optimal location. Their trade network spanned from Minnesota to the Pacific Coast and all the way to the Gulf Coast. Their primary commodities were furs, guns, and metals, but corn and other crops also passed through their marketplace.

The Hidatsas had their share of famous guests. The most well-known visitors were the members of the Lewis and Clark Expedition. During their stop at Awatixa in the winter of 1804–1805, they met the Shoshone teenager, Sacagawea, pregnant by her captor/husband and far from her homeland in the mountains. History records her as the woman who saved the expedition with the serendipitous encounter with her brother, guided the expedition through the Rockies, and traveled all the way to the Pacific Ocean. Other visitors included the artists George Catlin and Karl Bodmer, whose paintings of the Plains Indians' culture gave America their first tangible view of their neighbors.

The hospitality shown by the Hidatsa, though, nearly wiped them out. An 1837 smallpox epidemic, exacerbated by the trade business, killed half the villages' population. Accompanied by the neighboring Mandan and Arikara, the Hidat-

Canoeing the Missouri River near Knife River

sas relocated north, further upstream. The lodges, meant to last about a decade, collapsed, leaving the ripples in the ground visitors see today.

The National Park Service has worked to restore the prairie to how it looked when the Hidatsa lived here, planting cottonwoods, green ash, American elm, box elders, and other native trees near the rivers, and mostly treeless grassy prairie above the valley. While restoring Knife River to its former glory is extremely unlikely, the park honors its former inhabitants while helping us wonder what we have lost in the American conquest of North America.

How much hospitality to show a stranger is a charged issue these days. We are comfortable helping some strangers but not others, and at times we're not exactly sure what compels us to make those choices. But over and over, our faith calls us to welcome the stranger regardless of how different the stranger may be.

Prairie wildflowers

When has somebody shown you unexpected or undeserved hospitality? When have you shown hospitality toward somebody else? How do you decide who deserves hospitality and who does not?

HOPEWELL CULTURE
NATIONAL HISTORICAL PARK

OHIO • 1923 • HISTORY

I consider the days of old, and remember the years of long ago.
—PSALM 77:5 (NRSV)

At first glance, they look like rolling hills. Closer examination reveals something far more intricate and sacred than one might expect from a cluster of hills in south-central Ohio.

The present Hopewell Culture National Historical Park represents an expanded zone of preservation that began with the Mound City Group established in 1923 to include Hopetown Earthworks, High Banks works, Hopewell Mound Group, and Seip Earthworks. The Hopewell culture itself characterizes a group of prehistorical people of the Woodland Era in North America who existed during the first thousand years of the Common Era.

We don't know what these people actually called themselves, as they have left behind no known written language from which we can learn about them. The name *Hopewell* relates to the name of the Ohio landowner, Mordecai Hopewell, whose name was invoked by the first archaeologists excavating the mounds. Hopewell's name became associated with an entire culture of similar mound-building peoples that ranged over a large area of eastern North America.

The reconstructed earthworks are impressive in both scale and design, sometimes exceeding a height of 40 feet on a base 100 feet wide, with the diameter or length stretching as much to 1,600 feet. Mounds are most often geometrical—circular, square, rectangular, and octagonal. Their exact purpose remains a mystery, though they are thought to have been ceremonial centers, dwellings, or fortresses. Unfortunately, many mounds were destroyed by both the passage of time

Mound City Group from the air. The careful observer will note that the site is currently shared with a golf course.

A rainbow stretches over the Mound City Group.

through erosion and the settling of the land by pioneering Europeans who simply plowed them into farm fields. The Mound City Earthworks was razed in the early twentieth century to become Fort Sherman, an army training base in the First World War. It wasn't until the base was closed in 1922 that excavation and reconstruction began to take place.

Preserving these sites is a reminder that we are not the first to inhabit this land, and the archaeological study of what has been left behind tells us that, however primitive we may believe these ancient people were, they stood under these same stars, walked this familiar ground beneath us, and had similar questions about their place in all of it. They, too, wondered what came before them and they must have mused about what might follow. Could they ever have imagined the twenty-first century and what life might be like in their distant future that is our present?

The knowledge necessary to construct the mounds indicates that

Aerial view of Newark Earthworks in Heath, Ohio. Closer examination will reveal the octagon and circle mounds.

these people had significant knowledge of mathematics and engineering, as well as astronomy, since many of the structures align with lunar and/or solar cycles. To give you an idea of the scale of the construction, four structures the size of the Roman

Colosseum would fit inside the Octagon at the Newark Earthworks site.

Even though they apparently lived independently and not in large villages or within the walls of the structures they erected, the people of the Hopewell culture had a desire to come together. They apparently participated in a vast trading network, as items contained in the burial chambers below the mounds range in origin from the Yellowstone

A copper effigy found among the Mound City Group artifacts

basin (grizzly bear teeth) to the Caribbean (conch shells), the Great Lakes (copper) to the Appalachian Mountains (mica)—a distance of over 1,400 miles from southeast to northwest.

Many of the items that archaeologists have unearthed were buried with the dead, perhaps for them to remember or celebrate their past life; or, possibly as gifts of homage by those who would remember them, or to recognize some state of status achieved in their lifetime. The items represent high levels of craftsmanship, created from copper, stone, and bone.

Memory plays an important role in the biblical faith. Frequently God is beseeching the people to remember the goodness, faithfulness, and commands of God. More than that, the people are hoping God *won't* remember their own short memories of these same things! The very center of the Abrahamic faiths is built upon remembering the saving acts of God. For Jews, this is at the Red or Reed Sea, which recalls Israel's escape from Pharaoh; for Christians it is at the practice of the Lord's Supper, which recalls Christ's death and resurrection; for Muslims, it is in remembering the absolute nature of God in faithful observance of Muhammad's teachings.

Whose memory do you honor? Why is it important for communities to have common remembrances? How do you want to be remembered?

The 9:03 gate represents the beginning of recovery from the tragic Oklahoma City bombing.

OKLAHOMA CITY
NATIONAL MEMORIAL

OKLAHOMA • 1997 • INNOCENCE

"But nobody knows when that day or hour will come, not the heavenly angels and not the Son. Only the Father knows. . . . Therefore, stay alert! You don't know what day the Lord is coming."

—MATTHEW 24:36, 42 (CEB)

On Wednesday April 19, 1995, as usual hundreds of people entered the Alfred P. Murrah Federal Building in downtown Oklahoma City. Many of them worked in the nine-story structure that housed several federal agencies, but some were customers visiting the offices for everyday needs like getting a Social Security card or making a deposit at a credit union. The second floor housed a day care.

At 9:02 that morning, a massive truck bomb, detonated by a domestic terrorist, shattered the building, and shook the prairies for dozens of miles. A third of the Murrah Building collapsed. Within seconds, 168 people—including 19 children under the age of six—were killed in the explosion.

Within seconds, hundreds of local first responders poured into the disaster zone, risking their own lives to assist the more than eight hundred people injured by the blast and working to free those trapped in the rubble. In the following days, rescuers from across the country traveled to Oklahoma City, initially hoping to find survivors but eventually honoring the dead by retrieving their bodies.

Thirty-four days later, the building's remnants were imploded. Ton after ton of debris was hauled away, and eventually the site was cleared. Residents of Oklahoma City were adamant that the Murrah Building site would become a memorial to the 168 victims and a monument to those who risked everything to help their neighbors.

A warm summer night at the Oklahoma City National Memorial

Within eighteen months, a task force selected from more than six hundred entries a design by Hans and Torrey Butzer, and the federal government added the site to the National Park Service. The Butzers' design transformed a 3.3-acre site into a memorial that evokes sorrow and inspiration, sympathy and pride.

Where the building once stood now stand 168 chairs, each bearing the name of a victim, including smaller chairs for the children killed. The chairs are arranged in nine rows representing where the person had been in the building at the time of the explosion, with five additional chairs representing those who died in an adjacent building.

Where Fifth Street once carried traffic, a shallow pool lined with black granite now mirrors the ever-changing Oklahoma sky. The wind barely ripples the pool, always reflecting the park around it.

Where the eastern wall of the building withstood the blast now stands a plaque, etched into granite salvaged from the Murrah Building itself,

The Survivor Tree, an American Elm that miraculously survived the explosion

bearing the names of more than six hundred survivors of the bombing.

Where a parking lot had been, the Survivor Tree honors the spirit of the city and the country. An American elm estimated to be a century old, the Survivor Tree was nearly felled in the criminal investigation, and many assumed it would die soon. The following spring though, the tree bloomed, and the memorial is designed to protect the revered tree's roots for generations to come.

Bookending the block where the federal building once stood are the Gates of Time, bronze structures memorializing the times before and after the explosion. Their symmetry, one reading 9:01 marking the last moments of peace, the other 9:03 marking the beginning of recovery, can make time feel as though it is standing still.

Where there had been a fence protecting the crime scene now stands the Memorial Fence, a makeshift shrine where countless thousands have honored the victims and first responders in their own unique way, whether with art, stuffed animals, T-shirts, photographs, or other trinkets. To this day, items are still collected and stored.

Nestled into the north side of a growing downtown neighborhood, the Oklahoma City National Memorial is an oasis of peace where once there was unthinkable destruction and death. Visiting the memorial is more than a history lesson; it is an opportunity to reflect on how quickly our lives can end and how we may or may not be ready for the consequences, on earth or in heaven. It is also an opportunity to be grateful for those, like first responders, who protect us and endure the worst that humanity can offer, day in and day out.

Where in your life do you still have pockets of innocence? How can you help others protect the innocence they have? In what ways can you reclaim the innocence you have lost?

Field of Empty Chairs, individually remembering each of the 168 victims

Sheep Rock and the John Day River

JOHN DAY FOSSIL BEDS
NATIONAL MONUMENT

OREGON • 1975 • ANCIENT

"Where were you when I laid out the foundation of the earth?
Tell me if you understand."

—JOB 38:4 (NIV)

There is old, and then there is ancient.

Old can be a '57 Chevy, your great-grandfather's pocket watch, or a Gutenberg Bible. They are things we know something about because an oral or written historical context gives insight into them. There is corroborating evidence regarding its origin, who owned it, how it was used, what its value was, and how someone acquired it.

Ancient is something altogether different. If something is "really ancient," it likely predates written language or even human community itself. It may be beyond our direct knowledge, requiring educated assertions based on clues in the surrounding environment.

At John Day Fossil Beds National Monument, ancient is defined as up to forty-five million years old! Covering fourteen thousand acres, this basin in central Oregon provides a record of how the region changed, and how life, both plant and animal, changed with it. Just east of the Cascades, this basin exists within what geologists refer to as "ring of fire," an area of potent volcanic activity that circles the Pacific Rim. The ash, mud, lava, and minerals from millennia of belching eruptions, along with the changes in the environment and climate those eruptions caused over long periods of time, altered what could survive and eliminated what could not adapt.

The secrets hidden in the strata of the earth's crust lie beneath land that in the last five thousand years was home to the hunter-gatherers of the Wasco, Northern Paiutes, Warm Springs, and Umatilla

The fossilized skull of a *Miohippus,* an ancient horse

native peoples. Along the John Day River they competed for salmon, elk, and huckleberries to sustain themselves, mostly unaware of the record of time that lay under their feet. As American settlers came westward along the Oregon Trail, they preferred the Willamette Valley beyond the Cascades, so the area was sparsely populated through the 1840s. The Homestead Act of 1862 and its offer of free land attracted more settlers, who discovered the rich fossil beds along the river and surrounding areas.

Three strata covering eight unique time periods have been uncovered in three separate regions of the monument. These strata track the rise and adaptation of mammals from the time this part of Oregon was a hot and wet tropical rain forest forty-four million years ago, the Clamo Strata, to seven million years ago, when this now–partially high desert country was a thriving grasslands, the Rattlesnake Strata. The oldest animal fossils trace to thirty million years earlier, with the beginnings of wolves, tapirs, and alligators in the Clarno Nut Beds along with walnut, chestnut, banana, and palm trees. Relatives of the modern fox, horse, panther, pig and the mixed hardwood forest also make an appearance as early as forty-four million years ago!

The biblical witness suggests that the earth

Painted Hills, whose colors change as daylight shifts

is very old and that things have changed over time. In Genesis 6:4, prior to the great flood, we hear this strange reference: "The Nephilim were on the earth in those days, and also afterward, when the sons of God went in to the daughters of

Erosion has exposed countless fossils and carved a rugged landscape.

humans, who bore children to them. These were the heroes that were of old, warriors of renown" (NRSV). Other books, such as Ezekiel, Numbers, and Isaiah, refer to these ancient beings as "giants" or "terrifying warriors," and their origin and meaning, though well debated by scholars, remain unclear.

In the books of Job, Isaiah, and the Psalms, we learn of Leviathan, the great sea monster, which along with Behemoth is also mentioned in the deuterocanonical book of 2 Esdras. Were these actually great beasts that once roamed the waters, or are they metaphors for chaotic forces yet to be fully subdued? Could there have been others like them that once were but are no more? Faith leaves them as open questions shrouded in the mystery of Divine action in the past, and science seeks to provide answers about what might have been. In this regard, faith and science are more partners than adversaries as they both seek to understand that which is ancient and came before us. Science and theology are both quests to greater understanding about what we know and what we believe.

How has the old or ancient connected you to the past? What things about your own history help you understand yourself? What might you leave behind that would give insight into your life and values?

INDEPENDENCE
NATIONAL HISTORICAL PARK

PENNSYLVANIA • 1956 • LIBERTY

Proclaim LIBERTY Throughout all the Land unto all the
Inhabitants Thereof Lev. XXV. v X.

—LEVITICUS 25:10, KING JAMES VERSION, AS RECORDED ON THE BELL

It is a bell like no other, an iconic symbol of the American Revolution and the birth of this country's independence. But the name *Liberty Bell*, at the time it was cast, has more to do with the lettering found around its shoulder than the founding of our nation. After all, when the order for the bell to be cast was issued in 1751, America was still a colony under British rule and there were no overt plans for a revolution and "liberty" from England. The symbol of freedom it has come to represent would not find an association with the bell until nearly one hundred years after it first sounded.

The bell familiar to us is actually the third casting from the materials of the original bell, shipped from England in 1752 to hang on the Pennsylvania State House. When the bell arrived from its voyage, it cracked the first time it was sounded, prior to being hoisted up onto the roof. Local Philadelphia founders Pass and Stow, whose names now adorn it, volunteered to recast the bell. At its first public ringing, however, it made what observers said "was a most unpleasant sound," and revealed the founders' inexperience as bell makers. It was broken apart and recast. The third time being the charm, it rang in a more pleasing tone, and was thus hung in the bell tower in July 1753.

The bell rang for various purposes early in its life, including for the assembling of public meetings, temporarily calling a congregation to worship while the nearby church building was under construction. Despite legends to the contrary, the bell did not ring on July 4, 1776, as

Liberty Bell with Independence Hall in the background

From an 1856 publication of the Boston Anti-Slavery Society

the Declaration of Independence was not read publicly until July 8, 1776.

Remarkably, the origin of its famous crack is uncertain. There is no historical record of when the bell first suffered the trademark fissure, which may have occurred as early as 1817. It is pictured *uncracked* in a publication as late as 1837, but in 1846 the *Public Ledger* reports it had rung on the anniversary of George Washington's birthday "though it had long been cracked" and that it "fell forever dumb" after that date.

The words from Leviticus that ring the upper portion of the bell are words with the power to inspire. "*Proclaim liberty throughout the land unto all the inhabitants thereof.*" One need not proclaim liberty if freedom already exists. The statement announces that an emancipation long hoped for has come, or is coming soon. Perhaps that

1916 photo entitled: *Women's Suffrage. Liberty Bell for Suffrage*

is why the first known use of the image of the bell was not to celebrate independence but to promote the abolition of slavery. The 1837 publication mentioned above was from the Abolitionist Society, and the image of the Liberty Bell became associated with that movement until the Civil War.

During Reconstruction, and in celebration of the nation's centennial, the bell became a symbol for unifying the recently divided-and-reunited country. It toured the United States, traveling by rail from 1885 to 1915, to be seen by tourists in cities, expositions, and fairs. Later, while the bell was still making its way around the country, the women's suffrage movement cast a replica of the bell and chained the clapper of the reproduction to prevent it from ringing. They sought liberty of a different sort, the right to vote. The Nineteenth Amendment was ratified in August 1920, and the chain restricting the clapper was symbolically cut.

The bell would once again find its image used during the civil rights movement in the 1960s, working to fully realize the emancipation that American people of color had sought for a century. Who can forget Martin Luther King Jr.'s speech from the National Mall in Washington, whose impassioned plea was that we should "let freedom ring" for in doing so all of us, despite our diversity, "will be able to join hands and sing in the words of the old Negro spiritual 'Free at last, free at last; thank God Almighty we are free at last!'"

If liberty and freedom had a sound, what do you suppose they would sound like? What in your own life needs liberation and release? What systems or circumstances that hold people captive in your community can you help to alleviate?

Liberty Bell returns to Allentown, Pennsylvania, 1893.

Downtown Providence's Roger Williams
National Memorial

ROGER WILLIAMS
NATIONAL MEMORIAL

RHODE ISLAND • 1966 • RELIGIOUS FREEDOM

There is neither Jew nor Greek, there is neither slave nor free,
nor is there is there male and female, for you are all one in Christ Jesus.
—GALATIANS 3:28 (NIV)

The freedom to choose and practice a religion, without governmental interference, is one of the founding principles of our country. From an early age we are taught that the United States was founded by people seeking religious freedom. One of the earliest examples of religious conflict in our country centers on Roger Williams and our smallest state, Rhode Island.

Williams's story traces its roots to the split between the Roman Catholic Church and the Church of England in 1534. A century of efforts to appease both sides and to keep the peace left the conflict simmering. This is the religious climate in which Roger Williams, a young minster in his midtwenties, entered ministry in 1629.

Born in London in 1603 and a standout student at Cambridge University, Williams felt his Church of England was still too much like the other (Roman Catholic) church in its beliefs and practices. The Puritans were a better fit—but religious dissent was dangerous in those times, a crime punishable by death. Puritans soon began leaving England, and Roger and Mary Williams arrived in Boston in 1631.

Even then, Williams still found trouble. Boston colony was still closely aligned with the Church of England, so Williams headed north for the more theologically moderate colony of Salem—the same Salem that had alleged witch problems years later. That didn't work out, so he headed south to the separatist colony Plymouth, of Pilgrim fame. There, he befriended the neighboring Wampanoag and Narragansett tribes,

Statue of Roger Williams at the eponymous university

learning their languages and their way of life, which in turn opened his eyes to some of the un-Christian ways in which the English colonists treated their new neighbors. Williams became an advocate for the tribes, calling for the colonists' land to be returned to the tribes, but this didn't sit well with colony leaders. Charges were brought against Williams for his "new and dangerous opinions against the authority of the magistrates," and in 1635, the court ruled that he be deported.

Not one to let authorities dictate his actions, Williams instead fled the colony, setting out as winter arrived for the nearest European colony—New Amsterdam (today's New York) two hundred miles away.

As luck or perhaps Divine Providence would have it, he survived the trip. The Wampanoag found Williams, sheltered him, and took him to the home of a tribal leader. Trusting Williams more than the English, the Wampanoag allowed him to establish a colony on the eastern banks of the Seekonk River. When the Plymouth colonial leaders

Monument's main building and nearby Rhode Island State Capitol

learned of his presence, they advised him to cross the river, out of their jurisdiction. There he met a party of Narragansett, who shared the same warm feelings as their east-bank neighbors. Williams later wrote that, "having made covenant of peaceable neighborhood with all the sachems and natives round about us, and having, in a sense of God's merciful providence unto me in my distress, called the place *PROVIDENCE*, I desired it might be for a shelter for persons distressed for conscience."

Rhode Island thus became a refuge for religious freedom-seekers, reaffirmed in 1663 by a royal charter: Rhode Islanders could "freely and fully have and enjoy his and their own judgments and consciences, in matters of religious concernments."

Shade-filled oasis in downtown Providence

Today, Providence has about one hundred eighty thousand residents and is the home of Roger Williams National Monument. The small site contains one of Providence's oldest buildings, a park honoring the first Jewish person elected to a city public office, and another historic grove and garden—a monument to religious diversity and the preacher-settler who lived peaceably with his neighbors and instilled in the American consciousness the principle of freedom of religion.

One hundred fifty years later, that principle became the first line of the First Amendment: "Congress shall make no law respecting an establishment of religion, or prohibiting the free exercise thereof;" and that principle has made the United States one of the world's most diverse countries as regards religious belief. Yet we still struggle to balance where one person's freedom impinges on the freedom of another.

Cathedral of St. John and a historic marker

When have you felt unable to live your religious beliefs faithfully? Can you remember an instance when you kept someone from exercising his or her own religious beliefs? How do you reconcile where one person's rights begin to impede somebody else's rights?

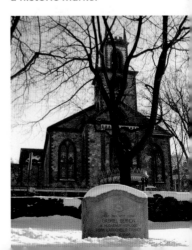

FORT SUMTER AND FORT MOULTRIE NATIONAL HISTORICAL PARK

SOUTH CAROLINA • 1948 • CONFLICT

For the Master, GOD-of-the-Angel-Armies,
is bringing a day noisy with mobs of people,
Jostling and stampeding in the Valley of Vision,
knocking down walls and hollering to the mountains, "Attack! Attack!"

—ISAIAH 22:5 (MESSAGE)

There is something unsettling about visiting battlefields even though today they are often peaceful, beautiful places with manicured landscaping dotted by memorials or perhaps tombstones. We read markers describing the battle that took place on that same ground, and we imagine the action while masking the carnage that took place there. Fort Sumter, South Carolina, challenges visitors with an even larger task: this is where the Civil War began.

Built as a coastal defense after the War of 1812, Fort Sumter occupied a small island near the mouth of Charleston harbor. A mile northeast was Fort Moultrie, dating back to the earliest days of the Revolutionary War. Together, the pair of forts, along with a seawall constructed from seventy thousand tons of New England granite, were to protect a key Southern port.

Sumter was to be a formidable structure, its walls fifty feet tall and five feet thick, bristling with 135 cannons that could reach any vessel attempting to enter the port. But construction was never completed, the fort never supplied. Across the harbor, Fort Moultrie was not easily defensible.

For almost three decades the forts went unused, but Lincoln's 1860 election changed that. A month later, South Carolina lawmakers

Battlements inside Fort Sumter

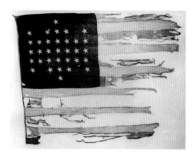

The original flag that flew over Fort Sumter during the siege and after its recapture

seceded from the Union and demanded that Union military installations surrender to the local militia. At Fort Moultrie, Major Robert Anderson refused, and on the day after Christmas 1860, he abandoned Moultrie and relocated his garrison to unfinished, unoccupied, and unsupplied Fort Sumter.

For more than three months, Anderson's troops encamped under siege at Sumter, anxiously watching the Confederacy grow and preparing for the outbreak of war. Knowing Union soldiers would run out of supplies in mid-April, Confederate forces rebuffed attempts to provide reinforcements and supplies.

After Anderson rejected a final demand of surrender, Confederate forces opened fire a few hours before daybreak on April 12, 1861. For the next thirty-four hours, shelling pounded the fort. Union forces didn't have the type of artillery needed to respond effectively, and the surrender of Fort Sumter appeared imminent.

Three miles northwest of the fort, Charleston residents watched the bombardment, some celebrating the outbreak of hostilities. Across the country, word of war spread rapidly, with some newspapers providing coverage within a few hours. While the country—or, at the time, the countries—knew more blood would be shed, many expected the conflict to last only a few months.

Fort Moultrie, one of America's first coastal fortifications

Astoundingly, not a single Union soldier died in the siege, and Anderson took advantage of an opportunity to abandon Fort Sumter rather than surrender his

soldiers. He agreed to a truce on the afternoon of April 13. During a ceremony handing the fort over to Confederates, two Union soldiers died when a gun exploded. History records Daniel Hough, an Irish immigrant, as the war's first fatality. Anderson took Sumter's battle-ravaged flag when he left the fort, and in the North it became a potent symbol of the conflict.

Two years later, Union forces attempted to reclaim Fort Sumter. The effort failed, but Union gunboats pounded the island for the remainder of the war, reducing it to rubble. After four long years of war, with Charleston back in Union hands, Anderson returned to Fort Sumter, and the same tattered flag he had lowered in 1861 once again fluttered over Charleston.

The Fort Sumter we explore now was rebuilt in the years following the war, and it was an active fort until 1947, when it was decommissioned and transferred to the National Park Service.

When people of faith consider what justifies armed conflict, most believe the American Civil War certainly qualifies—a just cause, a justifiable decision made by competent leaders, waged fairly, unavoidably necessary. We look back at the Civil War knowing its results: slavery abolished, the country preserved, a budding international power that often took the moral high ground. We know war and conflict have horrible consequences, but there are times when conflict is necessary to achieve something greater in our lives or our world, to bring justice and peace we crave and that God calls us to create.

When have you felt you had no choice but to enter a conflict? What conflicts in your life do you need to engage more intentionally or in a different way to be more effective? In what context can you be a peacemaker?

Fort Sumter from the harbor

MOUNT RUSHMORE
NATIONAL MEMORIAL

SOUTH DAKOTA • 1933 • LEADERSHIP

*"Do you understand what I have done for you?" [Jesus] asked them. "You call
me 'Teacher' and 'Lord,' and rightly so, for that is what I am. Now that I, your
Lord and Teacher, have washed your feet, you also should wash one another's
feet. I have set you an example that you should do as I have done for you."*
—JOHN 13:12–15 (NIV)

The sculpture would be so much bigger than life—American heroes
on a heroic scale. It would require an entire mountain of granite. Historian Doane Robinson knew the sculpture would draw visitors
from around the world to South Dakota's Black Hills.

Robinson's idea is not what you are imagining right now. The granite
Robinson had in mind was The Needles, and the heroes he envisioned
were explorers Lewis and Clark, showman Buffalo Bill Cody, and Oglala
Sioux warrior Red Cloud. Robinson pitched the idea to state leaders,
attached sculptor Gutzon Borglum to the project, and started raising money despite opposition from Native Americans who revered the
Black Hills. Borglum rejected The Needles' poor granite and opted for
another mountain five miles northeast, a mountain of gleaming white
granite that faced southeast—Mount Rushmore. The idea evolved into
honoring four presidents whose legacies shaped America: George Washington, Thomas Jefferson, Abraham Lincoln, and Theodore Roosevelt,
chosen by the sculptor because of their expansion and preservation of
the country. The vision was cast.

Work on Mount Rushmore began in 1927. Sculpting on such a scale
required brute force: dynamite took off the large pieces, and drills
"honeycombed" the rock to make smaller pieces removable by hand.
The first president's sixty-foot-tall face was the first to be completed

Mount Rushmore, distant for miles but instantly recognizable

Mount Rushmore before scuplting

in 1934 followed by Jefferson in 1936 (on the project's second try after the first attempt failed due to poor-quality rock), Lincoln in 1937, and Roosevelt in 1939. The original plan for the mountain had been to sculpt each character to the waist as well as noting the Declaration of Independence, the Constitution, and the Louisiana Purchase. Borglum's death in 1941 and dwindling funding brought an end to the project less than two months before Pearl Harbor dragged the United States into World War II.

During Mount Rushmore's construction, Lakota Sioux Henry Standing Bear envisioned a Native American response to Mount Rushmore, a response that in part reminds us that treaties gave the Black Hills to the Native Americans forever—only to see that pledge broken a few decades later. Since 1948, the Crazy Horse Memorial has painstakingly emerged from Thunderhead Mountain, about ten miles southwest of George Washington's profile. Like Rushmore, it intends to sculpt an entire mountain, this one 563 feet tall. Like Rushmore, much work remains.

Eight decades later, Mount Rushmore is truly iconic: a marvel of engineering, a symbol of leadership, and a metaphor for greatness. "Who's on your Mount Rushmore?" is contemporary shorthand for "Who do you believe is the greatest of all time?" From time to time, proposals pop up for adding a fifth face to Rushmore, but those proposals peter out. It will likely remain these same four presidents for our lifetimes.

It's difficult to dispute the influence the four presidents had on our country. Washington won the war that freed us from British rule and set the presidential standard. Jefferson doubled the size of the country, enhancing our chances of survival. Lincoln kept us united as a single country. Roosevelt led the conservation movement that protects our most treasured lands and natural resources. Each crafted a legacy that influences how we think about America and our jobs as Americans, even as we disagree about the ways we live into those beliefs.

Goldenpea, a common summer wildflower

In our own lives, we have our own Mount Rushmores. We know those who have affected our lives, who inspire us to greatness, who help us to see the possibilities of what could be. These might be our family, parents or grandparents or siblings or guardians who shaped our everyday lives. They could be teachers who helped us discover our educational strengths. They could be artists who inspired us to think creatively. They could be pastors or spiritual leaders who accompanied us as we discovered our unique place in the world. They could be the ones who love us, for better or for worse.

Who are the people who have shaped you into who you are today? What are your unique traits that you wish you could strengthen? How do you inspire others to find their talents or live better lives?

The famous scuplture emerging from fall fog

GRAPHITE REACTOR

LOADING FACE

The main attraction at Oak Ridge was the
X-10 Graphite Reactor.

MANHATTAN PROJECT NATIONAL HISTORICAL PARK

TENNESSEE, WASHINGTON, AND NEW MEXICO • 2015 • CHOICES

I call heaven and earth to witness against you today that I have set
before you life and death, blessings and curses.
Choose life so that you and your descendants may live.

—DEUTERONOMY 30:19 (NRSV)

The Manhattan Project represents the marvel of human ingenuity and the tragedy of human failings. This National Historical Park is actually in three places in three different states. It was so secret that even Harry Truman, vice president of the United States, did not learn about it until he took the presidential oath of office upon Franklin D. Roosevelt's death in April 1945. Less than four months later, Truman was forced to decide if, then how, to use the terrible destructive force that the Manhattan Project had produced.

Nuclear fission was discovered in Germany in 1938; within a year, Albert Einstein wrote to Roosevelt that he believed an extremely powerful bomb could be created from this process. In response, Roosevelt initiated federal funding for uranium research. By 1942, with the United States at war, researchers concluded a bomb was in fact possible and that it could be built in time to influence the outcome of the global conflict. Under the auspices of the Army Corps of Engineers, the Manhattan Engineer District was created. The project combined industrial, scientific, and military resources, employing thousands of people across the United States and Canada at a cost over twenty-three billion in today's dollars.

This project drew talent from the best minds in the country and abroad, many of whom had escaped Nazi Germany and its

Women played a signifcant role in the war effort, including the Manhattan Project at Oak Ridge.

European satellites. Tennessee's Oak Ridge site, under the command of Kenneth Nichols, produced and refined uranium for construction of the bomb. Across the country, plutonium was produced in a plant near Hanford, Washington, a second park location. This site and others employed women and people of color, unusual for a research and development project in pre-civil rights America. A Presidential Executive Order decreed that the pursuit to harness the power of the atom before our rivals required the best America had to offer—regardless of race, creed, color, or national origin. While it did not end the evils of racism or cement equal rights for women, the war effort tempered many social norms due to what was at stake in defeating the Axis powers. This choice would have a lasting impact for both women and nonwhites in post-war America.

The scientific achievements of the Manhattan Project cannot be underestimated. Yet the fallout of harnessing this power was significant. The United States is the only country to have used nuclear weapons. More than seventy years after the bombing of Hiroshima and Nagasaki, that decision is still hotly debated. It undoubtedly shortened the war in the Pacific, as the Japanese unconditionally surrendered a week after Nagasaki was bombed,

In spite of segregated conditions in the South, African American workers were crucial contributors to the project's success.

saving millions of lives of combatants and civilians from both sides.

Yet the choice to use this weapon raised difficult ethical questions and resulted in the Cold War, which consumed countless dollars and inestimable creativity from all of the countries involved.

However, a positive, though unintended, consequence of this choice was to advance other supporting technologies that took humans into outer space

This billboard greeted employees at the Oak Ridge site to remind them of the top secret nature of their work.

and improved innumerable scientific fields, from energy to medicine. Much good has come from harnessing the atom. It produces electricity and powers naval vessels, and radioactive isotopes help us diagnose and cure diseases. The hope is that we will use its power in peaceful ways.

Physicist J. Robert Oppenheimer oversaw the Manhattan Project from the scientific laboratory in Los Alamos, New Mexico, the park's third site. After the first successful test of the completed bomb, Oppenheimer considered words from the *Bhagavad Gita*: "Now I am become Death, the destroyer of worlds." He chose to help America win the race to split the atom and use its power to end the war. Later, he chose to be a voice to end global nuclear proliferation, and he publicly opposed the pursuit of more powerful thermonuclear weapons. It is not without irony that the choice that has kept nations with nuclear weapons technology from using it against each other is called the doctrine of MAD—Mutually Assured Destruction.

How do you choose between competing positive options that have potential negative outcomes? When has a choice you've made had unintended consequences? How do you use your own agency for the common good?

SAN ANTONIO MISSIONS
NATIONAL HISTORICAL PARK

TEXAS • 1983 • LEARNING

For learning about wisdom and instruction,
for understanding words of insight,
for gaining instruction in wise dealing,
righteousness, justice, and equity;
to teach shrewdness to the simple,
knowledge and prudence to the young—
let the wise also hear and gain in learning,
and the discerning acquire skill . . .

—Proverbs 1:1–5 (NRSV)

History increasingly acknowledges the loss of life, land, culture, language, and the right of self-determination that occurred when European colonists arrived in the New World of the Americas. The crown, the church, and later the government of the United States did irreparable damage to the people who first lived on these lands. The twenty-first century grants us the privilege of 450 years of perspective and critical thinking, providing a different worldview than those who erroneously considered themselves to be pioneers on new shores. We can't undo the past. However, by learning from it, we can choose not to repeat it, and contrition for the ill-chosen deeds of our ancestors is appropriate.

There were two different ways that colonial powers operated in the New World. The English and the French secured the land within their stated claims by importing colonists who were faithful to the ruling power, thus serving the interest of the crown. The Spanish, on the other hand, converted the existing population to become loyal to the monarchy and then to act on behalf of the Spanish empire in preserving

Bell tower of San Juan Church

Life-giving water for farming and ranching was provided by aqueducts such as the Espada.

and protecting the colony. Spanish missions recognized at San Antonio Missions National Historical Park were created to stop incursions by the French into what is now east Texas, and used the Christian faith to create new subjects to the Spanish realm.

The problem with the plan was that the Caddoan Indians of east Texas had little need for what the Spanish had to offer. The Caddo were well organized, enjoyed a wide trading network, and practiced sustainable agriculture; they were not interested in converting to the Catholic faith. Garnering little success, the missions moved westward in 1739 to the San Antonio River, where priests encountered hunter/gatherer tribes with lesser technologies who felt threatened by encroaching tribes such as the Apache. They were better candidates for the mission's agenda and its benefits.

While the principal aim of the missions was to increase the influence of the Spanish monarchy, there were many advantages provided to those who chose to live within these communities. Missions were essentially schools set up by the Spanish government and the church. Aside from the safety of living within the mission's walls, people who lived in them gained skills necessary to support a community, skills such as farming, animal husbandry, carpentry, masonry, weaving,

Convento Cloister at Mission Concepción

pottery, candle making, and soap production, along with technologies such as the aqueduct, irrigation, and iron working. All men were expected to learn a trade, and missions served as economic engines in their regions.

Water delivered over distance by aqueducts was controlled for irrigaton by acequia and gates like this one at San Juan Mission.

Visitors will find many surprises in San Antonio Missions Historic National Park. Atop the list is that the best known of the San Antonio missions, the Alamo, is not included in this park; the Alamo, revered as the birthplace of the state of Texas, is managed by the state itself. As much as Texas claims its cultural independence from Spanish culture, many images and words we find to be quintessentially "Texan" have Spanish origins. Many items we most associate with cowboys originated with Spanish *vaqueros*—words such as lasso, lariat, corral, rodeo, chaps, buckaroo, and mustang. And the Spanish reintroduced horses to North America. All of these actually came to Texas via Mexico.

The missions taught the Catholic faith and the discipline of "the hours." Life in the mission was dictated by "the bell," which called the community to wake, to work, to pray, to eat, and to rest. The success of the San Antonio missions is evidence that the people received the faith and practiced it. Embracing learning improved life for individuals, and the missionary's passion for teaching acknowledged God as the source of all good gifts, wisdom, and skill. The missions were not perfect, but neither were they devoid of value.

What skill or wisdom did you learn from a favorite teacher? What knowledge are you intentionally passing on to a younger generation? About what do you hunger to learn more?

Union Pacific 119 replica

GOLDEN SPIKE
NATIONAL HISTORICAL PARK

UTAH • 1957 • DETERMINATION

Do you not know that in a race all the runners run, but only one gets the prize?
Run in such a way as to get the prize.
—1 CORINTHIANS 9:24 (NIV)

A railroad stretching from one coast to another—was it even possible? Not that long ago, the idea seemed out of reach. Golden Spike National Historical Park is where the impossible became reality.

The idea of building a transcontinental railroad had been around since the 1830s, but it took California's 1850 admission to the Union to make the railroad a crucial project for the country's future. Even as a brand-new state, California already influenced national politics; its admission as a free state essentially blocked the expansion of slavery to the Pacific. Soon surveys mapped out an ideal route, but it took the eruption of the Civil War to propel those plans into action. Politicians recognized that a transcontinental railroad would both draw California closer to the free Union and enhance the postwar economic opportunities. Congress passed legislation during the war to create the Union Pacific and the Central Pacific railroads, with federal, state, and private financing to pay for it—as well as land rights along the tracks that the rail companies could sell to future settlers.

Union Pacific began their work at Council Bluffs, Iowa, heading west across the plains. The Central Pacific began near Sacramento, working east into the Sierra Nevadas. A third privately held company, the Western Pacific, connected Sacramento to San Francisco Bay.

The route traversed nearly two thousand miles, which would have been a daunting challenge even if those miles were tabletop flat.

Laying the final rail, 1869

This route had to climb up the imposing Rocky Mountains, cross barren deserts, and then descend to the Sierra Nevadas, much of it in relatively treeless terrain that wasn't conducive to operating fire-driven equipment.

War-driven shortages of material labor and logistical issues delayed major construction until 1865; even then, Union Pacific completed only fifty miles of track. Two years and about five hundred miles later, the track reached Cheyenne, Wyoming Territory. In the less-populated West, labor was harder to come by, so Central Pacific hired Chinese workers by the thousands. Eventually, four of every five Central Pacific workers were Chinese, about twelve thousand in all. The terrain was tougher too; they encountered a much steeper slope in the California mountains.

As the two rail lines approached each other at Promontory Summit in the Utah Territory, national excitement grew. On May 10, 1869, with the hammering in of a golden railroad spike, the two railroads were united. What had been a six-month trip across the continent by horse-drawn wagon could now be completed in a week.

A reeanctment of the Golden Spike ceremony

In all, the Union Pacific laid 1,085 miles of track, the Central Pacific 690 miles, and the Western Pacific 132 miles: more than 1,900 miles built in about four years.

In a country now crisscrossed not only by trains but also by interstate highways, and in an era in which we can board a plane and traverse the continent in less than a day, it's easy to forget the significance of what happened at Golden Spike National Historical Park. Today we can see replicas of the two train engines, the *Jupiter* and *No. 119*, that met at Promontory Summit, learn the history of the railroads, and, during the prime season, join a reenactment of the driving of the Golden Spike.

A jackrabbit checks out the sagebrush.

There is, of course, a dark side to the transcontinental railroad. It decimated Native American populations, nearly exterminated the American bison, and made a few early investors immensely wealthy. But it was a significant factor in making sure a growing country didn't split into several pieces.

Perhaps we can truly understand the significance of that continental connection when we consider the determination that went into creating the railroad. Surveyors scanned the countryside time and time again seeking the perfect routes. Engineers meticulously designed bridges to cross streams and canyons. Manufacturers crafted engines capable of pulling tons of freight uphill without breaking down or exploding. Thousands of laborers—many of who came to this country to take a grueling job for terrible pay—took pride each day in building several thousand feet of track. The determination of tens of thousands of people, working together, achieved what many deemed impossible. Determination is about change, making something new or different happen. Determination changes the world.

When in your life has your determination helped you power through a challenge? What are you determined to make happen in your life? How can you help somebody who is determined to make something important happen?

MARSH-BILLINGS-ROCKEFELLER NATIONAL HISTORICAL PARK

VERMONT • 1992 • STEWARDSHIP

"But ask the animals, and they will teach you;
the birds of the air, and they will tell you;
ask the plants of the earth, and they will teach you;
and the fish of the sea will declare to you.
Who among all these does not know
that the hand of the LORD has done this?
In his hand is the life of every living thing
and the breath of every human being."

—JOB 12:7–10 (NRSV)

Outside of Woodstock, Vermont, a legacy of stewardship stretches across three families and two hundred years. Charles Marsh, a Vermont attorney, built a home in 1805 where his son, George Perkins Marsh, later lived. George was also a lawyer and a politician who served as a diplomat for both presidents John Tyler and Abraham Lincoln. He understood that the fall of many great societies could be traced to their lack of caring for natural resources, so he developed a stewardship land-management system for the United States. His book *Man and Nature, or the Physical Geography as Modified by Human Behavior,* written in 1864 and updated in 1874, in part laid the groundwork for the modern conservation movement. He sought to preserve the natural environment but died before he was able to see his efforts materialize on a grand scale.

After his death, the property was purchased by Frederick Billings, who established a farm in keeping with Marsh's practices and ideals. Now a museum within the National Monument, the farm was later purchased by Laurance and Mary French Rockefeller, also committed to the conservation movement. Laurance served as an advisor to several

Summer brings full blooms to the formal gardens.

presidents on matters related to the stewardship of resources, and they gifted the property to the people of the United States in 1992.

The mission of the park is grounded around these words from Laurance:

> The true importance of Marsh, Billings, and those who follow in their footsteps, goes beyond simple stewardship. Their work transcends maintenance. It involves new thought and new action to enhance and enrich . . . the past. . . . We cannot rest on the achievements of the past. Rather each generation must not only be stewards, but activists, innovators, and enrichers.

The Marsh-Billings-Rockefeller National Historical Park serves as a model of community cooperation and investment, as well as park-management innovation and creativity. Rather than being defined simply by its boundaries, the community of Woodstock so embraces the park that through thirty miles of footpaths and hiking trails, it is hard to tell which is which. There is a deep commitment to teach the next generation to be faithful stewards of the land through the "forest in every classroom" program, bringing children into the woods not simply to learn, but to *experience* responsible forest management. The park's Forest Center focuses on preserving a working landscape within the timber industry and, at the time of its construction, was one of only three Platinum LEED (Leadership in Energy and Environmental Design) buildings in the park service. Marsh-Billings-Rockefeller also hosts the Stewardship Institute, a part of the Naitonal Park Service dedicated to using a

The annual peak to peak hike each fall challenges hikers to ascend both Mount Tom and Mount Peg the same day.

collaborative community approach to change, as a way to preserve and protect park service lands into the twenty-first century.

If you want to walk in the winter, prepare for the trek.

Stewardship is a concept that runs through the biblical witness from beginning to end. When human beings are commanded to have dominion in the earth, over the birds, fish, and land creatures, the intention is that they will rule in the world in a manner similar to the way God rules in the cosmos. The encouragement to "be fruitful and multiply" is assurance that there is enough to ensure generativity into the future. Managed well, there is a sufficiency for the creation not simply to survive, but to thrive. There is no room or permission for mindless exploitation, but rather a reminder to tend the garden for the benefit of all. This kind of faithfulness results in a successful and abundant future.

The lesson is clear: our very survival depends on how well we manage the earth on which we live. Can we live in partnership with nature in such a way that we can draw on the resources we need in sustainable ways that still protect the planet? To date, there are no other options, and the alternative to good stewardship leaves the future in serious doubt.

The Forest Center offers a look at responsible forestry and sharing the land's resources.

What gifts have been passed on to you from the past? How do you plan for the future? In the choices you make, how do you take into account your impact on the earth?

APPOMATTOX COURT HOUSE
NATIONAL HISTORICAL PARK

VIRGINIA • 1966 • MERCY

He has shown you, O mortal, what is good.
And what does the LORD require of you?
To act justly and to love mercy
and to walk humbly with your God.

—MICAH 6:8 (NIV)

Few could have predicted the outcome. For months, Ulysses S. Grant's army had laid siege to Richmond and Petersburg, two key Virginia cities, and to the Army of Northern Virginia under Robert E. Lee's command. In March 1865, supplies ran out, and Lee's army broke west for the Appalachians. Perhaps they could resupply and regroup, they thought. Or perhaps they could disappear into the mountains to wage a guerrilla war against Union troops or unite with another Confederate army.

For over a week, an exhausted, hungry, demoralized Confederate army limped west, Grant breathing down their necks. A skirmish at Sailor's Creek resulted in eight thousand casualties, including the capture of about one-fifth of the Confederate forces. Lee's army was in tatters, and he knew it. He was running out of options.

Grant's forces knew they had the advantage. They were larger, better supplied, and better fed than Lee's army. Beyond that, they knew that if they could cut off Lee's retreat, it could end the war. For Union soldiers, it would be easy to imagine ending the campaign with a bloodbath, killing every last Confederate soldier. Thousands would die on both sides, but the toll would be much heavier on the rebels.

But Grant didn't want that bloodbath, nor did his commander-in-chief. A few weeks before the surrender, Grant, President

The road out of Appomattox Court House

A postcard of Lee's surrender by Keith Rocco

Lincoln, and two other military leaders discussed how to end the war. Lincoln's heart "was tenderness throughout," wrote Admiral David Porter, "and as long as the rebels laid down their arms, he did not care how it was done." They agreed that a merciful approach was the right way to end the war.

Both Grant and Lee recognized the opportunity to save thousands of lives. Grant sent a letter to Lee entreating him to surrender, but Lee stood firm and kept scrambling west. A second letter, though, proposed meeting the next morning—Palm Sunday—in Appomattox Court House, a town of about fifty residents. This time Lee agreed.

The generals planned to meet in the home of Wilmer and Virginia McLean. Lee arrived on time, but Grant was delayed, so Lee rested beneath an apple tree before waiting in the elegant three-story brick McLean home. Once Grant arrived, they sat in the parlor, and Grant laid out the terms for Lee's surrender. The amicable meeting between two generals lasted about ninety minutes. When Lee left and rode back to his defeated army, an amazing armistice was in place.

Over the next few days, the Confederate Army prepared for their surrender. Following the terms that Lee and Grant had negotiated, soldiers handed over the rifles, the weapons of battle, but kept their sidearms. They could keep their horses and mules so they could plant

McLean House, site of Lee's historic surrender to Grant

spring crops back home. Each
soldier would receive a written
pass that would let them travel
home without Union interference. The following Wednesday,
the surrender took effect. The
bloodbath had been avoided. It
took until November for the last

Roadside wildflowers

Confederate military unit to capitulate, but Lee's surrender at Appomattox Court House is remembered as the end of the war.

Little did the generals on that Palm Sunday know what a tumultu-
ous Holy Week would follow. On Good Friday, Lincoln was shot, and
he died the next morning. A country celebrating victory and antici-
pating Easter had suddenly lost its leader. History changed directions
in ways that still affect our country.

Today in Appomattox Court House National Historical Park, the
McLean Home stands amid fields that could have become battlefields.
Visitors stand in the very room where the war ended and walk the fence-
lined road on which those soldiers took their first steps home. It is a
strangely holy place.

So much unexpected mercy was shown at the end of the Civil War
by both sides. Lincoln and Grant averted the massacre that would have
been a mighty victory. Lee accepted
surrender to spare countless lives. And
thousands of soldiers followed peaceful
orders. So often we have opportunities
to show mercy, and our faith calls us
to demonstrate that mercy abundantly.

Reconstructed Appomattox
County Courthouse

Who has shown you mercy? To
whom have you shown mercy to at a time
when mercy was not required? Is there
somebody who needs your mercy now?

Dry Falls, eastern Washington

ICE AGE FLOODS
NATIONAL GEOLOGIC TRAIL

WASHINGTON, IDAHO, MONTANA, AND
OREGON • 2009 • RECOVERY

The waters flooded the earth for a hundred and fifty days.
But God remembered Noah and all the wild animals and the livestock that were
with him in the ark, and he sent a wind over the earth, and the waters receded.

—GENESIS 7:24–8:1 (NIV)

The lore of many civilizations includes flood stories. The Judeo-Christian scriptures recall Noah and his family, spared because of their obedience to God. Babylonians tell of Gilgamesh, Hindus of Manu, the Muisca of Bochica. Stories of catastrophic floods can be found on every inhabited continent.

We may not think of the dry inlands of the Pacific Northwest as a flood zone, but it bears the distinct scars of dozens of massive floods dating back to between twelve and seventeen thousand years. And it's all because of glaciers. During the most recent ice age, glaciers reached into the northern continental United States. We can see their work at several National Park Service unit sites, including Glacier and North Cascades national parks.

Eastern Washington's strangely sculpted terrain, known as the Channeled Scablands, fascinated geologist J. Harlen Bretz. He suggested that the terrain results from unparalleled flooding, but most geologists dismissed the idea. Further east, fellow geologist Joseph Pardee looked up at the mountains over Missoula, Montana. There he saw level lines, indicating high-watermarks. Pardee followed these lines northwest to Sandpoint, Idaho, where they were replaced by U-shaped valleys, evidence of a glacier capable of blocking the river. A prehistoric dam and river melted away. Bretz and Pardee's work changed the

Sediment from Glacial Lake Missoula

fundamental understanding of our planet's geology.

An ice age glacier almost two thousand feet tall and thirty-one miles long dammed the Clark Fork River, which drains much of western Montana toward the Pacific. As temperatures warmed, glacial ice melted, but trapped upstream the water pooled, creating a lake spanning hundreds of miles with half the volume of Lake Michigan—no fishing pond this! Deep mountain valleys cut by streams now flooded transformed into what is now called Glacial Lake Missoula. Centuries later, the town of Missoula sits more than nine hundred feet below the historic waterline.

Eventually the glacier dam collapsed, and trillions of gallons of water gushed downstream—rapidly and intensely, with a powerful flow that would dwarf today's Amazon River, so much water it wouldn't be constrained by the meager Columbia River valley. The lake flooded over southeastern Washington's flatlands. The upper layers of eastern Washington's rocks are largely lava, relatively soft rock easily eroded by the incredible force exerted by the draining lake. The result was

Moses Coulee

the Channeled Scablands, two thousand square miles marked by steep-walled, flat-bottomed coulees, braided drainage channels, massive islands of soil and gravel, giant current ripples dozens of feet tall, huge out-of-place "erratic" boulders, and strange landforms like currents pushing water uphill.

The most mind-boggling

evidence of this flood is Dry Falls, a marvel even without water. Now a ledge four hundred feet above the valley floor, Dry Falls was incredibly wet, more than three miles long, and with up to ten times the combined flow of all the rivers we know now, rushing at 65 miles per hour. Remember that a current of ten miles per hour has the same force as a 270-mile-per-hour wind. This is no gentle stream!

The Glacial Lake Missoula flood wasn't a one-time event either; the glacier-damming and release of the Clark Fork happened dozens of times, every forty years, give or take, and it's possible that early-arriving Native Americans witnessed some of the events. Imagine seeing a wall of water rushing across dry land—a flood of biblical proportions.

Ice Age Floods National Geologic Trail traces the route these floodwaters took through the Pacific Northwest. Still under development, the trail will connect these different landmarks. Traveling downstream by canoe, then by car or bicycle, provides a sense of how catastrophic these floods were.

Eventually the threat of a massive flood subsided with the end of the ice age. We can see the scars of these catastrophes and how the land has recovered. When the waters receded, people started over as Noah's family did. We know recovery is possible, that life may be different but that life can go on, that our faith calls us to continue living even when the odds are overwhelming.

When have you had to recover from a disaster, natural or personal? Who supported you in your recovery? Whom do you know that could use some help recovering from personal struggles?

Lines etched on Mount Sentinel hint at the lake that once drowned Missoula, Montana.

Harpers Ferry, nestled between the
Shenandoah and Potomac rivers

HARPERS FERRY NATIONAL HISTORICAL PARK

WEST VIRGINIA, VIRGINIA, AND MARYLAND • 1963 • RESISTANCE

After entering the temple, [Jesus] threw out those who were selling and buying there. He pushed over the tables used for currency exchange and the chairs of those who sold doves. . . . The chief priests and legal experts heard this and tried to find a way to destroy him. They regarded him as dangerous because the whole crowd was enthralled at his teaching.

—MARK 11:15, 18 (CEB)

The ghost of John Brown still haunts Harpers Ferry.

What today is a small town tucked in the northeast corner of West Virginia was, in the years leading up to the Civil War, an industrial center on the Potomac River, the boundary between South and North. A federal gun factory and armory made a tempting target for the abolitionist Brown, one of the most controversial men in America for his violent Bloody Kansas crusade in 1856 to eliminate slavery on the western frontier. Believing only action, not endless debate, would end slavery, Brown concocted a plan to foment revolution among the slaves of Virginia.

Brown planned to pillage the armory, which may have held up to one hundred thousand guns, amass a volunteer abolitionist army, and quickly march deep into the South, providing the plundered guns to those who joined him. Brown truly believed his plan would work, and he and his followers prepared for the raid at a rented farm a few miles from the unsuspecting town.

On the evening of October 16, 1859, he launched his raid, seizing the armory and taking several hostages. Brown had planned to leave Harpers Ferry before word of the incursion reached the federal capital sixty miles down the Potomac. But a train conductor notified author-ities, a foreboding omen for Brown's army.

The tide turned quickly on Brown. Local militia and townspeople cut off his escape route and surrounded Brown inside a fire station. Brown's peace emissaries were killed, and federal Marines arrived under the command of Robert E. Lee, a Union general until 1861. Lee attempted to negotiate a peaceful end to the standoff, but Brown refused. A three-minute skirmish resulted in the capture of Brown and his raiders. In all, sixteen people died and nine were injured in Brown's ill-conceived plan.

Brown was tried for treason by a Virginia court and executed on December 2; six other raiders were executed in the following months. Harpers Ferry changed hands several times during the Civil War and was included in the northern portion of Virginia that seceded and became West Virginia.

That could mark the end of the story of resistance, but Harp-ers Ferry became the site of another revolutionary idea in the years following the Civil War. Storer College, a private college intended to be inclusive across lines of race and gender, was established in 1865. The idea of a college for African Amer-icans in Harpers Ferry was not universally accepted, and history tells of the harassment of teach-ers by residents and by the Ku Klux Klan. Storer College with-stood the intimidation, and local attitudes to the college's presence eased.

Steps to St. Peter's Roman Catholic Church

In 1906, the college hosted the second gathering of the Niagara Movement, an early civil rights movement led by W. E. B. Du Bois and William Monroe Trotter. Desiring active opposition rather than a more passive approach supported by leaders like Booker T. Washington, the Niagara Movement called for an end to segregation and Jim Crow laws that

Bolivar Heights

disenfranchised blacks. The civil rights movement that transformed American culture in the twentieth century and that is still working today for equality and justice can trace its roots back to Harpers Ferry.

After the landmark *Brown v. Board of Education* ruling that integrated public schools, Storer closed its doors in 1955. The National Park Service acquired the campus in 1962, and Storer now serves as an NPS training facility and a reminder of its founders' vision for justice.

One hundred fifty years after his death, John Brown is viewed as a martyr for the abolitionist cause— but also as a zealot who went too far. The same was said of the leaders of the Niagara Movement. While those leaders' ideals and tactics may have seemed extreme at the time, there is no denying that America is a far more just country because of their work and sacrifice.

Autumn splendor on
Loudoun Heights Trail

When have you heard the call to resistance in your life? What forces in your life need to be resisted now? How can you help others resist oppression?

APOSTLE ISLANDS
NATIONAL LAKESHORE

WISCONSIN • 1970 • LIGHT

Indeed, you are my lamp, O LORD, the LORD lightens my darkness.
—2 SAMUEL 22:29 (NRSV)

The twenty-two islands off Wisconsin's Bayfield Peninsula were created as the last continental ice sheet retreated, filling with melting ice the basins that their own movement had carved, and creating the Great Lakes. These islands sit on the southwestern shore of Lake Superior, the world's largest freshwater lake, a cold and unforgiving body of water that produces waves in excess of thirty feet high. In winter, the temperature can dip to minus 40 degrees Fahrenheit. This portion of the lake along the Crozet Archipelago has claimed more than its share of ships; the shallow shoals and stone outcroppings have proven too difficult for ships seeking refuge from the fury of Superior's open waters to navigate.

With the 1855 opening of the Soo Locks, connecting Lake Superior to Lake Huron, a market for the area's iron ore was created to the east as far as the St. Lawrence Seaway, and shipping increased significantly. Lighthouses were built to aid with navigation, six of which are in the Apostle Islands preservation area and the National Register of Historic Places. Many lighthouse historians consider this to be the best-concentrated collection of lighthouses in the country.

This National Lakeshore, which includes twenty-one of the twenty-two islands, also boasts wonderful biodiversity with over six hundred species of plants and an island full of black bears! Among its most unique features are sandstone caves, strikingly beautiful when winter decorates them with frozen waterfalls and icicles. Kayakers, boaters, and fisherman share the water, though the cold temperatures of the lake discourage

Devils Island from Lake Superior

The Outer Island lighthouse still warns ships of venturing too close to shore.

swimming. Put on a wetsuit and diving tanks, and the aforementioned shipwrecks await your curiosity in Superior's clear waters. Many of the islands and the wilderness area along the shore have campgrounds and places to hike.

Enjoying the rugged appearance of the islands leads one to imagine what it was like for the first people who inhabited this ground. Evidence suggests a prehistoric human presence as early as one hundred years before the birth of Christ, with indications of a more complex society and trading network by the year 950. The Anishinaabe people gave way to the Ojibwa, who developed special tools for agriculture, fishing, and hunting this land. They dominated the Lake Superior region and encountered the first French trappers in 1640. French missionaries gave the Apostle Islands their current identity, most likely named for twelve larger islands and the twelve apostles of Jesus.

European immigrants forced the Ojibwa off the land in the nineteenth century. They took the land, denuded the islands of their old growth forests, and overfished the waters that were already under stress from the invasion of lamprey (eel) from the Atlantic Ocean.

Because the islands are remote, the only year-round inhabitants, particularly on the smaller islands, were lighthouse keepers. They often brought their families to live with them as a buffer against the long and lonely passage of time, but human contact was still limited. Lightkeeping was a hard and sacrificial task, yet it was crucial to the safety and protection of those who sailed Superior's waters. That shaft of light in the darkness was, for many a mariner, the difference between life and disaster.

Light has remarkable properties. It can heal, it can warm, it can sterilize. It be can used to signal, to illumine, to cast shadows; it can pass through a vacuum; and until it is absorbed by something, it seemingly goes on forever! Without light, life itself would not be possible. We cannot imagine a world without it.

Perhaps that is why the image of light became so important to faith communities in seeking to describe the nature and influence of the Divine. In the Judeo-Christian traditions, light symbolizes Truth, God, Jesus, wisdom, the holy, purity, the spirit, knowledge, en*light*enment, awareness, and goodness. Light gives direction and reveals the nature of all things. It contrasts with darkness, which represents chaos and the absence of these things. And in faith stories, the people who follow God are themselves called to reflect the light of the Divine, or even at times to be the light in the world's darkness—in essence, to be lightkeepers.

How do you shine light into the darkness? How has your spiritual path been enlightened? To whom do you look as light in a time of distress?

Apostle Island caves in winter make for excellent exploring and unique beauty.

Circle of Sacred Smoke, by Junkyu Muto, framing Devils Tower

DEVILS TOWER
NATIONAL MONUMENT

WYOMING • 1906 • SACRED

Moses brought the people out of the camp to meet God, and they took their place
at the foot of the mountain. Mount Sinai was all in smoke because the LORD had
come down on it with lightning. The smoke went up like the smoke of a hot
furnace, while the whole mountain shook violently.

—EXODUS 19:17–18 (CEB)

You recognize it the instant you see it. Flat-topped, deeply grooved Devils Tower juts out of the Wyoming foothills, a stump of a mountain almost 1,300 feet above the Belle Fourche River valley. It's a rock climber's dream, a photographer's patient subject, a nature lover's odd delight. Devils Tower is so striking, Theodore Roosevelt made it the first national monument in 1906.

Fifty million years ago, Devils Tower was a laccolith—magma injected between two layers of water-deposited sedimentary soil. That magma solidified, and between five and ten million years ago, wind and rain eroded the soil around the igneous rock. What remains is a strikingly bizarre sculpture towering over the plains. These days, in the gorgeous Wyoming sunrises and sunsets, shades and shadows and perspective render a different view every time you look up.

Hundreds of deep cracks line the sides of the monolith, giving the tower its striking look. Different tribes tell different stories, each entertaining and insightful about their originating cultures, about how the grooves were created, but there is a common element: a powerful bear, giving chase, clawed the rock. Geologists, though, assert that the cooling lava created the oddly geometrically shaped grooves as it contracted.

Today, visitors can trek the fairly level, 1.3-mile long Tower Trail around the base, weaving through a pine forest and rocks that tumbled

Prairie dogs check out the visitors near their burrow.

from above. Each year, about five thousand rock climbers edge their way up in the grooves, relying on their own strength and smarts—a challenging but rewarding climb to the flat summit, roughly the size of a football field. Climbing up takes about five hours, give or take an hour; rappelling down takes about ninety minutes.

Devils Tower had its red-carpet moment in the 1977 sci-fi hit *Close Encounters of the Third Kind*, the location where humans and alien visitors first met. The movie is still celebrated; for years, the campground at the base has shown the movie for tourists. There truly is something thrilling about seeing the movie where filming actually took place.

Sprawling around the tower are high, dry, grassy prairies and the animals and plants that call the environment home. A favorite roadside stop is a colony of prairie dogs, popping up out of their burrows, dodging back in, reemerging elsewhere, a live-action game of whack-a-mole. Other plains dwellers, such as deer, rabbits, coyotes, red and gray foxes, bobcats, and mountain lions also frequent the park, along with at least eleven species of bats that nest in the cracks of the rock and the surrounding forest.

Native American prayer cloths and bundles

For countless years, Native American tribes such as the Arapaho, Crow, Cheyenne, Shoshone, Kiowa, and Lakota regarded the monolith as sacred ground. Each tribe in turn had its own name, in its own language: Mato Tiplia, Bear's Tipi, Home of the Bear Tree Rock, Great Gray Horn, Gray

Horn Butte. Before white settlers renamed it, Bears Lodge was the most common name for the monolith. Historians believe an 1875 surveying team misunderstood their Native American interpreter, hearing "Bears Lodge" as "Bad God," then Americanized the term to Devils Tower (which, without the apostrophe, is itself a grammatically flawed interpretation). Action by the federal government would

Columns curving at the tower's base

be required to change the name, an unlikely prospect anytime soon.

Regardless of its legal name, more than twenty tribes hold the tower as sacred, and the signs of this respect are all around when you walk the Tower Trail. Colorful prayer bundles, prayer cloths, and ribbons placed by pilgrims adorn the trees surrounding the tower. Visitors are asked not to touch these sacred symbols. Because many tribes believe scaling the monolith is disrespectful, the National Park Service instituted a voluntary moratorium on climbing during June, when many tribes mark the summer solstice and other sacred rituals. In the two decades since the policy was implemented, the number of climbers is significantly lower in June, meaning climbers recognize the holiness of the space—a tangible recognition of interfaith respect.

Ponderosa pines and grasslands surrounding Devils Tower

What have been or are the sacred places in your life? What makes those places sacred to you? How can you show respect for the places and objects others believe to be sacred?

Pictured Rocks National Lakeshore in Michigan

BENEDICTION

*When Solomon had finished the temple of the LORD and the royal palace,
and had succeeded in carrying out all he had in mind to do in the temple of
the LORD and in his own palace, the LORD appeared to him at night and said:
"I have heard your prayer and have chosen this place for myself as a temple for
sacrifices. . . .Now my eyes will be open and my ears attentive to the prayers
offered in this place. I have chosen and consecrated this temple so that my Name
may be there forever. My eyes and my heart will always be there."*
—2 CHRONICLES 7:11–12, 15–16 (NIV)

*"I am what time, circumstance, history, have made of me, certainly,
but I am also, much more than that. So are we all."*
—JAMES BALDWIN, AMERICAN AUTHOR AND ACTIVIST

*"The land, the earth God gave to man for his home . . . should never be the
possession of any man, corporation, (or) society . . . any more than the air or
water. Laws change; people die; the land remains."*
—PRESIDENT ABRAHAM LINCOLN

*"We come and go, but the land is always here. And the people who love it and
understand it are the people who own it—for a little while."*
—WILLA CATHER, AMERICAN AUTHOR

*"Never before have we had at hand so much knowledge of nature.
Our perception of reality is shifting on so large a scale there's no telling where
it's going. Nor can we have any idea how our behavior will change each time we
recreate nature within us. For all practical purposes, our changing perceptions
really are changes within nature itself. Still, our belief that nature has some
ultimate character, without us to witness it, keeps us honest.
It forces us to keep stretching and changing what we see."*
—JOHN H. LIENHART, AMERICAN ENGINEER AND WRITER

"The American way of life consists of something that goes greatly beyond the mere obtaining of the necessities of existence. If it means anything, it means that America presents to its citizens an opportunity to grow mentally and spiritually, as well as physically. The National Park System also provides, through areas that are significant in history and prehistory, a physical as well as spiritual linking of present-day Americans with the past of their country."
—NEWTON B. DRURY, NPS DIRECTOR

"Of all the questions which can come before this nation, short of the actual preservation of its existence in a great war, there is none which compares in importance with the great central task of leaving this land even a better land for our descendants than it is for us."
—PRESIDENT THEODORE ROOSEVELT

"There is nothing so American as our national parks. The scenery and wild life are native and the fundamental idea behind the parks is native. It is, in brief, that the country belongs to the people; that what it is and what it is in the process of making is for the enrichment of the lives of all of us. Thus the parks stand as the outward symbol of this great human principle. . . . a great recreational and educational project—one which no other country in the world has ever undertaken in such a broad way for protection of its natural and historic treasurers and for the enjoyment of them by vast numbers of people."
—PRESIDENT FRANKLIN DELANO ROOSEVELT

"The wilderness holds answers to questions man has not yet learned to ask."
—NANCY NEWHALL, AMERICAN WRITER

"Neither the life of an individual nor the history of a society can be understood without understanding both."
—C. WRIGHT MILLS, AMERICAN SOCIOLOGIST

"People don't take trips . . . trips take people."
—JOHN STEINBECK, AMERICAN AUTHOR

"The man who goes alone can start today; but he who travels with another must wait till that other is ready."
—HENRY DAVID THOREAU, AMERICAN AUTHOR

"Our national heritage is richer than just scenic features; the realization is coming that perhaps our greatest national heritage is nature itself, with all its complexity and its abundance of life, which, when combined with great scenic beauty as it is in the national parks, becomes of unlimited value."
—GEORGE MELENDEZ WRIGHT, NPS BIOLOGIST

"Who will gainsay that the parks contain the highest potentialities of national pride, national contentment, and national health? A visit inspires love of country; begets contentment; engenders pride of possession; contains the antidote for national restlessness. . . . He is a better citizen with a keener appreciation of the privilege of living here who has toured the national parks."
—STEPHEN T. MATHER, NPS DIRECTOR

"But, in a larger sense, we can not dedicate—we can not consecrate—we can not hallow —this ground. The brave men, living and dead, who struggled here, have consecrated it, far above our poor power to add or detract. The world will little note, nor long remember what we say here, but it can never forget what they did here. It is for us the living, rather, to be dedicated here to the unfinished work which they who fought here have thus far so nobly advanced."
—ABRAHAM LINCOLN, GETTYSBURG ADDRESS

RESOURCES

A couple of times each year a newspaper article appears featuring somebody who has visited each and every National Park Service unit. We are, frankly, quite jealous. Visiting each unit would, of course, be the trek of a lifetime and the best way to research this book. We were not able to do this. And for this, we are very, very sorry, both for the things we still have to learn and because this would be so much fun!

The next best way to research this book is to research, research, research, and that has been almost as much fun. An exhaustive bibliography would fill this book and crowd out the good stuff, so here are the resources that were most helpful:

+ Literature from the sites. Maps, brochures, trail maps—we each have a stockpile in the basement.
+ NPS.gov and its incredibly rich content. Most of the photos in this book are available on NPS.gov and are in the public domain. Thank you to the often-unnamed photographers who produced these breathtaking images. Additionally, we couldn't have done this without NPS.gov's wonderful descriptions, insight, photographs, multimedia, maps, and historical insights.
+ Park rangers. Admit it: You want to be a park ranger. So do we.
+ Wikipedia's many pages on national parks and related pages. While not a primary source, Wikipedia was a great way to confirm an accurate memory or correct an inaccurate one. It also pointed us to new primary information. Wikipedia is a great bibliography.
+ A slew of history books we've read over the years.
+ The "America's National Parks Podcast."
+ *The 10 Best of Everything: National Parks* by Robert E. Howells, Olivia Garnett, Gary McKetchnie, Jeremy Schmitt, Mel White, and Joe Yogurst (Washington, D.C.: National Geographic, 2011). If we got something wrong, please blame us, not the source.

PHOTO CREDITS

NPS.gov's extensive photo archive does not always list the photographer, nor does it consistently list whether the photographer was working for the National Park Service when the photo was taken. The credit below reflects how photo credits are (and are not) listed on NPS.gov. Photos by the authors and from Shutterstock are copyrighted, and all rights are reserved. Photos from Wikipedia were shared by their photographers — thank you! All other photos are in the public domain. Regardless of who took the photos and in what capacity they were working, on this we can agree: These photos are holy gifts! Thank you for your work.

Tall columns at Devils Tower National Monument, Wyoming

Transform Your National Parks Experience

AMERICA'S HOLY GROUND

61 FAITHFUL REFLECTIONS ON OUR NATIONAL PARKS

BRAD LYONS & BRUCE BARKHAUER

9780827200753

Now your national park experience can be a holy experience too. *America's Holy Ground* features inspiring spiritual reflections and nearly 200 breathtaking photos from every beloved national park to help you reconnect with God and the holy on your national park adventure. Each entry includes a scripture verse, and reflection questions to take your experience deeper. Blank journaling pages at the end make this book a keepsake.

"Its photos capture everything from the immense power and grandeur of rock, cavern, and ocean to the delicacy of a fragile bloom and the refreshing silence of deep forests. These, joined with historical information, Native American wisdom, contemporary science, and Bible-based devotions, make this lovely book perfect for collecting or gifting."
—*Foreword Reviews*

"...these ruminations on American national parks ... invite readers to appreciate the value of protected places and ponder their spiritual power." —*Publishers Weekly*

 chalice press

You Want to Change the World. So Do We.